The Meaning of Freedom

The Meaning of Freedom

Angela Y. Davis

Foreword by Robin D. G. Kelley

OPEN MEDIA SERIES | CITY LIGHTS BOOKS
San Francisco

Open Media Series Editor: Greg Ruggiero

Cover photograph © Keba Konte

Special thanks to David Barsamian and Alternative Radio

This book is also available as an e-edition: 978-0-87286-586-0

Library of Congress Cataloging-in-Publication Data
Davis, Angela Y. (Angela Yvonne), 1944–
 The meaning of freedom / by Angela Y. Davis ; with a foreword by
Robin D. G. Kelley.
  p. cm. — (Open media series)
 ISBN 978-0-87286-503-7
1. United States—Social conditions—1980- 2. United States—Politics
and government—1989- 3. Liberty. 4. Racism. 5. Civil rights. I. Title.
II. Series.

HN59.2.D38 2009
305.896'073—dc22

2009023359

City Lights Books are published at the City Lights Bookstore,
261 Columbus Avenue, San Francisco, CA 94133.
www.citylights.com

Contents

Foreword

By Robin D. G. Kelley

What is the meaning of freedom? Angela Davis's entire life, work, and activism has been dedicated to examining this fundamental question and to abolishing all forms of subjugation that have denied oppressed people freedom. It is not too much to call her one of the world's leading philosophers of freedom. She stands against the liberal tradition of political philosophy, the tradition derived from Hobbes and others that understands freedom as the right of the individual to do what *he* wishes without fetters or impediments, as long as it is lawful under the state. This "negative" liberty or freedom places a premium on the right to own property, to accumulate wealth, to defend property by arms, to mobility, expression, and political participation. Davis's conception of freedom is far more expansive and radical—collective freedom; the freedom to earn a livelihood and live a healthy, fully realized life; freedom from violence; sexual freedom; social justice; abolition of all forms of bondage and incarceration; freedom from exploitation; freedom of movement; freedom *as* movement, as a collective striving for real democracy. For Davis, freedom is not a thing granted by the state in the form of law or proclamation or policy; freedom is struggled for, it is hard-fought and transformative, it is a participatory process that demands new ways of thinking and being. Thus it is only fitting that she is among the few major contemporary thinkers who takes seriously Karl Marx's 1845 injunction that "The philosophers have only interpreted the world, in various ways. The point, however, is to change it."

Angela Davis was born and raised in apartheid Birmingham, Alabama, under conditions of extreme and blatant unfreedom. She grew up in the 1940s and '50s, when black middle-class homes were being firebombed regularly by white supremacists with the blessings and encouragement of police chief Eugene "Bull" Connor, and when black opposition to racism eventually brought the city to a standstill. She was nurtured by activist parents whose best friends were members of the Communist Party, and she came of age amidst a community in struggle. By the time she enrolled in New York City's Elisabeth Irwin High School (nicknamed the Little Red School House for its left-leaning philosophy) in 1959, she had already contemplated the meaning of freedom and understood that the question was no mere academic exercise. The quest for freedom drew her to radical philosopher Herbert Marcuse, with whom she studied at Brandeis University. It drew her to the writings of Baudelaire, Rimbaud, and Jean-Paul Sartre, and to France, where she studied abroad. During her stay in Paris, Davis developed an even more global perspective on the quest for freedom by witnessing the French racism against North Africans and the Algerian struggle for liberation. And, sadly, it was in France, in September of 1963, that she learned of the bombing of Birmingham's 16th Street Baptist Church and the murder of her childhood acquaintances, Denise McNair, Addie Mae Collins, Carole Robertson, and Cynthia Wesley. Their deaths wedded her to a life of struggle. She knew then, contrary to Jean-Paul Sartre's assertions, that there was no freedom in death. Freedom is the right to live, the necessity to struggle.

Davis continued her studies dedicated to producing engaged scholarship. With Marcuse's support and encouragement, Davis pursued her doctorate in philosophy at Johann Wolfgang Goethe University in Frankfurt, Germany, with the intention of studying with Theodor Adorno, but by this time Adorno had little interest in engaged scholarship. (Her model at Goethe University was a young professor named Oskar Negt, who never shrank from political engagement and actively participated in the Sozialistischer Deutscher Studentenbund [SDS].) West Germany was too far from the sites of engagement that most mattered to Davis, so after two years she returned to the states to resume her doctoral studies under Marcuse's direction at the University of California, San Diego.

The year was 1967, and it seemed as if every aggrieved group—youth, women, people of color—identified with liberation struggle. Freedom was in the air, and Davis threw herself mind and body into the movement. The rest of the story is quite familiar: her path from the Black Panthers to UCLA and her tangle with Governor Ronald Reagan, to Soledad Prison and the subsequent campaign that forever associated her name with Freedom. As an incarcerated political prisoner, she became the center of an international movement whose supporters pinned their own freedom to Davis's, concluding that to "Free Angela" was a blow to the blatant acts of state violence and unfreedom that crushed protests at the Democratic National Convention in 1968, that murdered Salvador Allende in Chile, that justified the dropping of napalm and herbicides on villages as far away as Vietnam and Mozambique. And like so many incarcerated revolutionary intellectuals, such as Antonio Gramsci, Malcolm X, Assata Shakur, George Jackson, and Mumia Abu-Jamal, she produced some of the most poignant, critical reflections on freedom and liberation from her jail cell.[1]

Davis's trial, subsequent acquittal, and struggle to find

work in the face of ongoing political repression have only reinforced her commitment to engaged scholarship, her explorations of the meaning of freedom, and her radical abolitionist politics. Even if one is not familiar with her leadership in the Communist Party USA, her role in the founding of the Committees of Correspondence, Agenda 2000, and Critical Resistance, or her prolific body of scholarship—from her collection *Women, Race, and Class* on the politics of reproduction, domestic violence, rape, and women and capitalism; her stunning *Blues Legacies and Black Feminism: Gertrude "Ma" Rainey, Bessie Smith, and Billie Holiday* on the politics of black women's expressive culture; to her more recent manifestoes calling for the end of the prison-industrial complex, *Are Prisons Obsolete?* and *Abolition Democracy*—the speeches published here prove the point.

Delivered between 1994 and 2009, these public talks reveal Davis further developing her critique of the carceral state, offering fresh analyses of racism, gender, sexuality, global capitalism, and neoliberalism, responding to various crises of the last two decades, and always inviting her audiences to imagine a radically different future. They demonstrate the degree to which she remains a dedicated dialectical thinker. Davis has never promoted a political "line," nor have her ideas stood still. As the world changes and power relations shift from a post-Soviet, post-apartheid, post-Bush world to the mythical "post-racial" one, she challenges us to critically interrogate our history, to deal with the social, political, cultural, and economic dynamics of the moment, and to pay attention to where people are. In the 1990s, she challenged parochialism and creeping conservatism in black movements; told us to pay attention to hip hop and the sigh of youth struggling to find voice; and warned us against nostalgia for the good old days of the 1960s when, allegedly, resistance movements had more leverage and enemies were easier to recognize. And she consistently takes on the prison-industrial complex. Davis frequently returns to the relationship between the formation of prisons and the demand for cheap labor under capitalism, and their unbroken lineage with the history and institution of slavery in the United States. Her powerful critiques of Foucault and other theorists/historians of the birth of the prison reveal the centrality of race in the process of creating a carceral state in the West. The critical question for Davis centers on how black people have been criminalized and how this ideology has determined black people's denial of basic citizenship rights. Since most leading theorists of prisons focus on issues such as reform, punishment, discipline, and labor under capitalism, discussions of the production of imprisoned bodies often play down or marginalize race.

While Davis's earlier speeches and many of the later ones could not have anticipated the election of Barack Obama, all of her words are incredibly prescient and relevant. Most pundits and commentators were quick to declare jubilantly that Obama's ascent to the presidency marked the end of racism. Color-blindness has triumphed, 'nuff said. Indeed, there is no need to even invoke the "r" word. Moreover, because Obama has been portrayed in such heroic light and his victory treated with such great symbolic importance for the African American community, to criticize or challenge the president is often regarded by liberal Democrats (especially black folk) as an act of disloyalty. But as Davis said in one of her speeches: "We're hardly two years into the Clinton presidency, and we seem to have forgotten how to organize masses of people into resistance movements. Many black people feel obliged to stick with Clinton through thick and thin, now don't they? We seem to have fallen prey to some kind of historical amnesia." And again, in 2009, as Obama continues a version of Bush's military tribunals, decides to hold some of the 9/11 detainees indefinitely, escalates the war in Afghanistan, avoids prosecuting U.S. officials responsible for torture, proceeds to bail out banks, and offers parenting workshops in lieu of restoring federal public assistance for the poor, we seem to be suffering from recurring amnesia. Obama promised to return us to the good old days when the Democrats occupied the White House, but as Davis reminds us, President Clinton's top priorities were the anti-crime bill and the elimination of welfare; there was no discussion of full employment or creating jobs. She also reminds us that it was the Democratic Senator Carol Moseley Braun who introduced the provision to try young teenagers as adults, thus contributing to the increase in the number of children in the state and federal prison system.

Moreover, Davis has long challenged neoliberal claims that we've achieved a color-blind society. She reminds us that any outbreaks of blatant, explicit racism are "now treated as individual and private irregularities, to be solved by punishing and reeducating the individual by teaching them color-blindness, by teaching them not to notice the phenomenon of race." In one fell swoop, social institutions and state practices are relieved of responsibility. To our peril, Davis warns, the vast majority continues to ignore the fact that the dramatic increase of people of color locked in cages is a manifestation of institutional forms of racism—from the inequities of mandatory minimums to the War on Drugs, racial profiling, and employment discrimination, to name a few.

Never one to shy away from unpopular positions, Davis offers a brilliant and timely critique of the struggle for equality by subjugated groups. What does it mean, for example, for gays and lesbians to demand the right to enter the military and to serve in every capacity without a critique of the institution's inherent and deep-seated sexism and homophobia? She asks the same of marriage—it is one thing to challenge any and all discriminatory barriers; it is another to interrogate the institution itself. The push to legalize gay marriage is growing by leaps and bounds now, but as early as 2008 Davis explained to an audience in Boulder, Colorado: "The structures of heteronormativity and the various violences these structures and discourses entail, do not necessarily disappear when the sexuality of the participant is changed. I'm not suggesting that we do not claim the right of gays and lesbians to engage in this practice, but we also have to think about the institution itself. It is an economic institution. It is about property. It is not about relations! Not about human relations, or intimate relations."

Finally, we must acknowledge that in the aftermath of 9/11, when many on the Left openly supported the war in Afghanistan and softened their position on U.S. military policy, Davis's position never wavered. From the outset, she delivered a blistering critique of Cheney and Bush's War on Terror, though it was an unpopular position to take immediately after the attacks on the Pentagon and World Trade Center. She critiqued the erosion of civil liberties, the racial profiling of Arabs, Muslims, and South Asians, and the imposition of an oppressive "security state" fueled by fear-mongering. And she questioned the patriotic turn, the resurgence of nationalism and all of its patriarchal trappings. She asks, "Why the nation?" The nation is constituted through exclusion, and after 9/11 "Americans" were not encouraged to identify with other people outside the nation, with the victims of torture, with Iraqis, with Africans and Asians, with others who might also have suffered from the aftermath of 9/11. Unfortunately, despite President Obama's assertion that he is a "citizen of the world," he, too, invoked "nation first" and set out on a foreign policy path that is not radically different from that of his predecessors. He continues to support a softer version of the expansionist, neoliberal, and militarist policies that have driven the last half-century of U.S. foreign policy. He certainly does not intend to limit American military power.

Ironically, Obama's election initially had the effect of virtually eliminating social movements from our public discourse. Although grassroots organizing made his election possible, all of our national discussions of policy focus on the president's individual decision-making to the exclusion of the demands of aggrieved groups. This is also affecting the way history is conceived in the popular consciousness: The New Deal of the 1930s, the foundation of the social welfare state, is now treated as the brainchild of Franklin Delano Roosevelt, not the product of struggles between capital, labor, civil rights organizations, communists, socialists, feminists, and the unemployed. Likewise, Abraham Lincoln, Obama's other alter ego, is represented to the public as the man who single-handedly ended the institution of enslavement in this country. Even Lyndon Johnson is credited with giving us the Civil Rights Act of 1964. In every case, it is the combination of great men and the law that supposedly generates radical social change, not social movements, not the imaginations and actions of ordinary people. But, again, Davis warns against fetishizing the law as markers of freedom. She reminds us that the Thirteenth Amendment did not abolish slavery, and it did not abolish all forms of coerced labor. While President Obama characterizes the United States as a "nation of laws," laws do not produce or guarantee freedom.

We still need abolitionists. And we still need an engaged

citizenry to organize, agitate, and challenge injustice with movements for change. The year 2011 seemed to give birth to just that: a new wave of global uprisings, rebellions, riots, organizing, and mass movements. In the United States, the wave took form in the unexpected emergence of the Occupy movement, and ever since the first demonstrators settled into New York's Zuccotti Park, Angela Davis has been a powerful spokesperson for, and presence within, the movement. From New York to Philadelphia, from Oakland to Berlin, the people's mic has projected her words to the indignant crowds of people challenging the ascendance of Wall Street and the privatization of what's left of our public institutions. Davis reminds the Occupiers that in our efforts to hold Wall Street accountable for the economic collapse, we must not lose sight of the bigger objective: a new society. In every speech, she envisioned freedom in ways diametrically opposed to the Friedrich von Hayeks, Milton Friedmans, and Larry Summerses of the world—a vision of an inclusive community founded on justice, and equality; the provision of education, health care, and housing; and the abolition of the carceral/police state. She also warned crowds that such a vision of collective freedom requires a radical conception of community. It's one thing to come together in parks and public squares, in streets and the halls of Congress. It is another thing to stay together and remake our relationships with one another. "Our unity must be complex," she often says when addressing Occupy gatherings. "Our unity must be emancipatory. It cannot be simplistic and oppressive." In other words, freedom is a process of becoming, of being able to see and understand difference within unity, and resisting the tendency to reproduce the hierarchies embedded in the world we want to change.

Ultimately, the speeches gathered together here are timely

and timeless. They embody Angela Davis's uniquely radical vision of the society we need to build and the path to get there. She still believes in social movements, in the power of people to transform society, and in a non-capitalist path. As she told an audience in 2005, the nation and the world are filled with "people who are not afraid to dream about the possibility of a better world. They say that a non-exploitative, non-racist, democratic economic order is possible. They say that new social relations are possible, ones that link human beings around the globe, not by the commodities some produce and others consume, but rather by equality and solidarity and cooperation and respect."

So all you out there who are not afraid to dream, who wish to end all forms of military occupation, corporate dominance, hierarchy, and oppression: listen, read, and heed the call.

ONE

Report from Harlem

Columbia University, New York City
September 9, 1994

I would like to thank the Institute for Research in African American Studies for having brought together an impressive group of black activists and scholars, not only from throughout this country, but from all over the world: Africa, Europe, the Caribbean. We are charged with the task of collectively reflecting on the theoretical and practical implications of political agendas taken up in black communities during this last decade of the twentieth century.

Negotiating the Transformations of History

It is good to be in Harlem on the thirtieth anniversary of Freedom Summer, one of the most extraordinary moments in the history of the black freedom struggle. Many of us (at least those of my generation and older) tend look back upon that period with nostalgia. Sometimes we veteran activists simply yearn for the good old days rather than prepare ourselves to confront courageously a drastically transformed world that presents new, more complicated challenges. We evoke a time when masses of black people, Latinos, Native Americans, and Asian Americans, along with our white allies, were on the move, determined to change the course of history. But instead of seeing past struggles as a source of inspiration impelling us to craft innovative approaches to contemporary problems, we frequently replace historical consciousness with a desperate nostalgia, allowing the past to become a repository for present political desires. We allow the present to be held captive by the past.

More than once I have heard people say, "If only a new Black Panther Party could be organized, then we could seriously deal with The Man, you know?" But suppose we were to say: "There is no Man anymore." There is suffering. There is oppression. There is terrifying racism. But this racism does not come from the mythical "Man." Moreover, it is laced with sexism and homophobia and unprecedented class exploitation associated with a dangerously globalized capitalism. We need new ideas and new strategies that will take us into the twenty-first century.

What I am suggesting is that those of us who are elders have to stop functioning as gatekeepers. We cannot establish age and civil rights or black power experience as the main criteria for radical black political leadership today. How old was Dr. Martin Luther King when he became the spokesperson for the Montgomery bus boycott? He was 26 years old. How old was Diane Nash? How old was Huey Newton? Fidel Castro? Nelson Mandela? Amilcar Cabral? Jacqueline Creft? Maurice Bishop? As for myself, I was only 25 years old when I had to confront Ronald Reagan over the issue of my right as a Communist to teach at UCLA. We cannot deny young people their rightful place in this movement today or it will be our downfall. In many instances, young people are able to see far more clearly than we that our lives are shaped by the intersections of race, class, gender, and sexuality. Those of us who are older have a great deal to learn from our younger sisters and brothers, who are in a better position than we are to develop the political vocabulary, the theory, and the strategies that can potentially move us forward.

These last three decades, many years of which have been devoted to intense struggles and sacrifices, have certainly produced victories. Who could have imagined in 1964, when Fannie Lou Hamer tried to gain entrance for the Mississippi Freedom Democratic Party into the Democratic Party convention, that we would have been able to elect forty black people to Congress, including a black woman to the U.S. Senate? And even more important, who would have imagined that this black woman in the Senate, heir to Fannie Lou Hamer, would sponsor one of the most repressive provisions of the recent crime bill? You see, it is no longer a question of simply resisting The Man. Circumstances are far more complicated than they used to be, or than our perceptions of them used to be.

We speak today about a crisis in contemporary social movements. This crisis has been produced in part by our failure to develop a meaningful and collective historical consciousness. Such a consciousness would entail a recognition that our victories attained by freedom movements are never etched in stone. What we often perceive under one set of historical conditions as glorious triumphs of mass struggle can later ricochet against us if we do not continually reconfigure the terms and transform the terrain of our struggle. The struggle must go on. Transformed circumstances require new theories and practices.

The Cuban Revolution is three and a half decades old. Holding on to a strong vision of socialism in the aftermath of the collapse of the socialist community of nations requires strategies that are very different from previous revolutionary struggles—from the attack on the Moncada barracks and the landing of the *Granma* to the triumph of the revolution. But the struggle does go on. Those of us whose radical consciousness and political trajectories were fundamentally shaped by Che, Fidel, Camilo Cienfuegos, and Juan Almeida have a special responsibility to stand with our Cuban sisters and brothers during their most difficult period. The embargo must end, and it must end now!

The South African struggle has entered a new phase. Many of us fought for Nelson Mandela's freedom during a substantial portion of our political lives. We protested the apartheid government's repression of South African Freedom Fighters while Mandela survived the brutal conditions of his imprisonment. Today Nelson Mandela is free, and he is president of a new South Africa. This new South Africa is striving to be free, democratic, non-racist, non-sexist, and non-homophobic. The struggle for freedom continues. This victory is not forever guaranteed. If we associated ourselves with the dismantling of apartheid, we should find ways to help shore up that victory today, and tomorrow, and the next day. We often are so captivated by the glamour of revolution that when pivotal though less glamorous moments arise, when our solidarities are needed more than ever, we fail to generate suitable responses. Let us not forget how quickly the revolution in Grenada was brought down by the assassinations of Maurice Bishop and Jacqueline Creft and by the U.S. military invasion.

This brings me back to the earlier point I made about our collective failures to negotiate historical transformations. Some of us remain so staunchly anchored to the discourses and strategies of earlier eras that we cannot adequately understand contemporary challenges. We fail to apprehend the extent to which theories and practices that were once unambiguously progressive become, under changed political circumstances, regressive and flagrantly reactionary. While we do need to be genuinely concerned about the growth and visibility of black conservatism (from Clarence Thomas on the Supreme Court to Phyllis Berry Meyers, who along with other black conservatives, played a key role in reversing the nomination of Lani Guinier for the Department of Justice's Assistant Attorney General for Civil Rights). At the same time we need to beware of the insinuation of conservative ideologies in what is publicly acknowledged as forward-looking strategy for black liberation. Beware of those leaders and theorists who eloquently rage against white supremacy but identify black gay men and lesbians as evil incarnate. Beware of those leaders who call upon us to protect our young black men but will beat their wives and abuse their children and will not support a woman's right to reproductive autonomy. Beware of those leaders!

And beware of those who call for the salvation of black males but will not support the rights of Caribbean, Central American, and Asian immigrants, or who think that struggles in Chiapas or in Northern Ireland are unrelated to black freedom. Beware of those leaders! Regardless of how effectively (or ineffectively) veteran activists are able to engage with the issues of our times, there is clearly a paucity of young voices associated with black political leadership. The relative invisibility of youth leadership is a crucial example of the crisis in contemporary black social movements.

On the other hand, within black popular culture, youth are, for better or for worse, helping to shape the political vision of their contemporaries. Many young black performers are absolutely brilliant. Not only are they musically dazzling, they are also trying to put forth anti-racist and anti-capitalist critiques. I'm thinking, for example, about Nefertiti, Arrested Development, The Fugees, and Michael Franti (whom I have been following since Disposable Heroes of Hiphoprisy). Cultural and political imagination like theirs may help shed light on our present dilemma and perhaps guide us out of the worst situation black people have faced in this century.

I need not mention the deeply misogynist and homophobic themes that seriously weaken hip hop's oppositional stance. Before, however, we identify hip hop as the main adversary on this account, let us remind ourselves that our ideological universe is saturated with patriarchal and heterosexist assumptions.

Clinton, the Crime Bill, and Race

We are not yet two years into the Clinton presidency and the possibilities of oppositional politics vis-à-vis the state have steadily diminished. Black people play a major role in immunizing the Clinton presidency against mass critique. It is as if black people felt obliged to stick with Clinton through thick and thin. We seem to have forgotten how to assume stances of opposition and resistance, how to identify submerged racial codes and markers, how to recognize racism even when the conventional markers are no longer there. This ability has historically earned African American activists a special place among people of color worldwide, and among people of all racial and national backgrounds. What used to be a sophisticated appreciation of racism seems to be collapsing. In the aftermath of the collapse of socialism, and in the context of many problematic regimes throughout Africa, how can we extol Bill Clinton as a symbol of radical change? This is deeply problematic.

In the August 29 issue of *Jet* magazine there is a revealing article about a birthday party for Clinton organized by a coalition of black, Asian, and Latino Democrats. Approximately 1,500 people of color attended that party, and an unprecedented $1.2 million was raised. According to the article, "For most minorities, President Clinton still was 'the main man,' holding to a commitment when human rights issues seem to have lost their glow." The fact that black people, along with Asian Americans and Latinos, could raise more than one million dollars in one evening should indicate to us that the political landscape has fundamentally changed. It should indicate to us that class configurations within the black community have undergone an important metamorphosis over the last two decades.

Contrast that million-dollar party with the situation that prevails here in Harlem. Some of us are far wealthier than we ever dreamt we would be. But far greater numbers of us are ensconced in a poverty that is far more dreadful than we could have ever imagined three decades ago. The film *Blade Runner* evokes the dystopian future of black inner cities—not only in Los Angeles but in East Oakland, Harlem, and the South Bronx—throw-away zones.

The *Jet* article praises Clinton for his many black appointments: Mike Espy, Ron Brown, and three others to his cabinet and more than five hundred black people to other posts in his adminstration. The article also praises Clinton for "boldly pressing for the nation's first health care and anti-crime bill." In fact, Clinton has established the crime bill as his number-one political priority, even more important than health care. Why was he so resistant to the single-payer initiative in health care? Why was this crime bill more important than a jobs bill? The last extensive discussion on full employment was the Humphrey-Hawkins Full Employment Act in 1978. Consider also that Clinton's proposed welfare reform legislation will force women on welfare to work after two years of receiving welfare payments. But where will they find jobs?

In the aftermath of the Cold War, the most important priority should have been to convert the wartime economy that had consistently drained the country of jobs, created structural unemployment, and led to the development of a structurally unemployed group of people in the black community and other communities of color, into a peacetime, full-employment economy. In 1994, why is it so easy to forget full employment, health care, education, recreation? Why is there such widespread acceptance of Clinton's law-and-order posturing? When the Republican Nixon first raised the cry of law and order, black people had no difficulty understanding the racial codes of that slogan. When the Republican Bush and his anti-crime campaign presented Willie Horton as the archetypal criminal—a black, male rapist and murderer of a white woman—it required no extraordinary intelligence to grasp the discursive link between crime and blackness.

Today, however, Clinton, a Democrat, who received proportionately more votes from the black community than from any other group of people in this country, is lauded as the quintessential warrior against crime, with his shrewdly racist policies divested of all explicit racial content. Intentionally making no direct allusions to race, Clinton employs a rhetoric that focuses on victims of crime. The quintessential contemporary victim is the white girlchild Polly Klaas. Please don't misunderstand me. Her murder was horrible, and I convey my sympathy to her parents. What I criticize is the rhetorical manipulation of her image as a crime victim. Clinton constantly has evoked Polly Klaas, and did so in the aftermath of the initial stalling of the crime bill. Although the suspect in the Polly Klaas case is a white man, there is enough socially constructed fear of crime entangled in the national imagination with the fear of black men that Richard Allen Davis, the white suspect, becomes an anomaly perceived as one white face representing a sea of black men who, in the collective mind's eye, comprise the criminal element.

This recently passed crime bill allocates over $30 billion

over the next six years to protect "us" from the criminals. Read the racial codes embedded in the discourse around the crime bill. They have become infinitely more complicated, and a good number of black people have been led to believe in the inherent criminality of certain groups of African Americans. They, like people of other racial backgrounds, need protection from these black criminals. The crime bill authorizes $8.8 billion over the next six years to put 100,000 new policemen and women on the streets of cities across the country; $7.9 billion in state construction grants for prisons and boot camps; $1.8 billion to reimburse states, which are encouraged to incarcerate more undocumented immigrants from Central America, the Caribbean, and Asia.

Ever greater numbers of people will be herded into prison and under the three-strikes-you're-out initiative; they will receive ever longer sentences, both in the state and the federal system. Ironically, under the provision introduced in the Senate by its first black woman member, Carol Moseley Braun, it will be easier to try young teenagers as adults. As a result we will soon have children in the state and federal prisons as well. There are already one million people in prison in the United States. This does not include the 500,000 in city and county jails, the 600,000 on parole, and the three million people on probation. It also does not include the 60,000 young people in juvenile facilities, which is to say, there are presently more than *five million* people either incarcerated, on parole, or on probation. Many of the people who are presently on probation or on parole, would be behind bars under the conditions of the recently passed crime bill.

So, you see, even without the draconian measures of the crime bill, black people are already 7.8 times more likely to go to prison than are white people. If we have any doubts about the move away from conceptualizations that prioritize rehabilitation as an aim of incaceration, consider the fact that prisoners will no longer be eligible for Pell Grant assistance for higher education. Not only is the duration of imprisonment drastically exended, it is rendered more repressive than ever. Within some state prison systems, weights have even been banned.

Having spent time in several jails myself, I know how important it is to exercise the body as well as the mind. The barring of higher education and weight sets implies the creation of an incarcerated society of people who are worth little more than trash to the dominant culture. The crime bill does not impact just the black community, it has consequences for Latino communities, Native American communities, Asian communities, Arab communities, poor white communities, and immigrants.

As black scholars and activists, our analysis and concerns should extend beyond what we recognize as black communities. Our political communities of struggle embrace all people of color—black, Latino, Asian, indigenous—as well as the poor in this country. The very same conditions of globalization that have robbed the black community of so many jobs have also led to increased migration into the United States. Capital migrates from country to country in search of cheap labor, and in the process it opens up circuits of human migration into this country. But now, according to the crime bill, the federal government will fund the incarceration costs of undocumented immigrants. We will all end up in the same place, whether we're African Americans, Haitians, Cubans, Latino Americans, Salvadorans, Mexicans, Chinese, Laotians, Arabs, so we'd better figure out how to build a resistance movement together.

Who is benefiting from these ominous new developments? There is already something of a boom in the prison constrution industry. New architectural trends that recapitulate old ideas about incarceration such as Jeremy Bentham's panopticon have produced the need to build new jails and prisons—both public and private prisons. And there is the dimension of the profit drive, with its own exploitative, racist component. It's also important to recognize that the steadily growing trend of privatization of U.S. jails and prisons is equally menacing. With this new crime bill, the Corrections Corporation of America, which is currently the largest company in the prisons-for-profit business, is very likely to grow. The union-busting trend that characterizes transnational capital is used by private prisons to cut their costs. Thus Corrections Corporation of America disallows unionization in its prisons. Moreover, its employees have no pension plan.

What was most worthy of note in the debate on the crime bill was that the black caucus insisted throughout on the inclusion of a racial justice act that would permit death-row defendants to use race as a mitigating factor. Unfortunately, that provision failed to be included. We therefore ask: How many more black bodies will be sacrificed on the altar of law and order? Why has it been so difficult to openly address issues of the social construction of race? Why haven't we more effectively challenged Clinton's erasure of race in the law-and-order rhetoric he has inherited and uncritically embraced? Perhaps because during the Reagan-Bush era the discourse on crime had already become so implicitly racialized that it is no longer necessary to use racial markers. What is troubling about the Clinton rhetoric is that the racisms that were so obvious in the law-and-order discourse of previous eras are becoming increasingly unrecognizable.

A New Abolitionist Movement

Dilemmas of law and order lurk in the background of discussions on black and Latino community anti-violence activism. When a child's life is forever arrested by one of the gunshots that are heard so frequently in poor black and Latino communities, parents, teachers, and friends parade in demonstrations bearing signs with the slogan "STOP THE VIOLENCE." Those who live with the daily violence associated with drug trafficking and the increasing use of dangerous weapons by youth are certainly in need of immediate solutions to these problems. But the decades-old law-and-order solutions will hardly bring peace to poor black and Latino communities. Why is there such a paucity of alternatives? Why the readiness to take on a discourse and entertain policies and ideological strategies that are so laden with racism? Ideological racism has begun to lead a secluded existence. It sequesters itself, for example, within the concept of crime. People who are deeply affected by the epidemic of violence understandably want to see an end to crime. But rarely do they have access to ideas other than those underlying retribution as justice. This is why it is so difficult to discuss possibilities of abolishing jails and prisons. I, for one, am of the opinion that we will have to renounce jails and prisons as the normal and unquestioned approaches to such social problems as drug abuse, unemployment, homelessness, and illiteracy.

In the nineteenth century, Thomas Malthus made assertions about the inexorablity of poverty. He argued that wars, natural disasters, and disease were natural ways of reducing poverty, which he assumed was just as unavoidable as the diseases, disasters, and wars that resulted in the deaths of so many human beings. Just as capitalism has naturalized poverty, crime is similarly naturalized. If crime is inevitable, then there must be more police and more prisons. Black scholars can support abolitionist strategies in ways that will lead to constructive bridge-building with other social movements. In this sense, it is time to explore approaches to decriminalization, especially decriminalization of drug use and prostitution.

When abolitionists raise the possibility of living without prisons, a common reaction is fear—fear provoked by the prospect of criminals pouring out of prisons and returning to communities where they may violently assault people and their property. It is true that abolitionists want to dismantle structures of imprisonment, but not without a process that calls for building alternative institutions. It is not necessary to address the drug problem, for example, within the criminal justice system. It needs to be separated from the criminal justice system. Rehabilitation is not possible within the jail and prison system.

One possible strategy, one that is supported by radical criminologist Pat Carlen, is to begin with women, who constitute a relatively small percentage of the country's and the world's imprisoned population, but who are most frequently convicted of such charges as drugs, prostitution, and welfare fraud. A policy of decarceration, especially for women who are convicted of so-called "nonviolent offenses" could result in the closing down of many women's jails and prisons. The resources thus liberated could be more productively used to develop educative and rehabilitative institutions. The successful elimination of women's prisons might then set a precedent that could be applied to men's facilities as well.

If decarceration and abolition are dismissed as too radical, then the only alternative will be to to continue incarcerating the black population in greater and greater numbers. If trends continue, as a result of the crime bill 50 percent of young black men could be behind bars in ten years time. And in another twenty-five years it might be as much as 75 percent.

What I'm suggesting is that dangerous limits have been placed on the very possibility of imagining alternatives. These ideological limits have to be contested. We have to begin to think in different ways. Our future is at stake.

Black scholars and activists, for example, need to learn how to engage in discussions that fearlessly point to the virulence of racism. We have to learn how to analyze and resist racism even in contexts where people who are targets and victims of racism commit acts of harm against others. Law-and-order discourse is racist, the existing system of punishment has been deeply defined by historical racism. Police, courts, and prisons are dramatic examples of institutional racism. Yet this is not to suggest that people of color who commit acts of violence against other human beings are therefore innocent. This is true of brothers and sisters out in the streets as well as those in the high-end suites.

The difficulty of acknowledging that an individual can be simultaneously acknowledged as a target of racism and as a perpetrator of injury was evident in the Clarence Thomas–Anita Hill story. Many who charged racism felt compelled to defend the person whom they perceived to be the target of racism. Certainly there was racism at work in the way the Senate Democrats staged the hearings. After all, it was Clarence Thomas, not Ted Kennedy, who was taken to task for his misogynist behavior. Black congressperson Mel Reynolds, who was recently indicted for sexual assault on a 16-year-old campaign volunteer, has attempted to avoid discussion of sexual abuse by insisting that he has been made a target of racism. Of course racism enables such exposés. But this does not, and cannot, serve as a justification of assaults on women—especially by black men who are in positions of power. We cannot allow our recognition of the racism that permeates economic and political institutions to obscure the pervasiveness of sexual harassment and abuse in black communities—poor as well as affluent.

The process of identifying racism does not always exonerate the victim.

Accountability remains. Brother Ben Chavis, for whose freedom I passionately fought on several continents, must still be held accountable for his exploitative behavior toward women. I love the brother and certainly appreciate the leadership he gave to the NAACP—I joined the NAACP for the first time in my life when he became its executive director. But I want to know, for example, why there were not more women on the senior staff? A victim of racism can also be a perpetrator of sexism. And indeed, a victim of racism can be a perpetrator of racism as well. Victimization can no longer be permitted to function as a halo of innocence.

Consciousness of Race, Class, Gender, and Sexuality
One of the major challenges in black, Latino, Asian, and Native American communities is to develop a popular consciousness of the complex relations of race, class, gender, and sexuality. In both scholarly and activist circles, we have been discussing the interrelatedness of these mode of oppression for more than a decade, but our politics continues to be driven by outmoded discourses and conceptions. As racism is on the rise, so are classism, sexism, and homophobia. Affluent black people are more willing than ever before to write off their poor, oppressed sisters and brothers. These are the same black folks who often claim to be victims of racism themselves when they don't get a promotion, but who won't even think about about supporting the custodial staff's right to unionization.

With respect to gender, many of us are held captive by masculinist perceptions of the black community that dangerously trivialize black women's place. Black men continue to be evoked as "an endangered species" while black women are seen as responsible for the reproduction of poverty-stricken fatherless families, whose male children are destined to become prison statistics. Black women who dare to think that they can build families without men are represented as destroying the community. In this framework of ideological misogyny, black women are perceived as the reproducers of violent black men. Within discussions on African Americans in higher education, the increasing percentage of black women receiving PhDs is often viewed as pathological. It is as if our problems would magically be solved if only black women recognized their traditional place and agreed to stand behind their men.

This discourse on saving young black men is often pervaded with sexism and misogyny. Women continue to be represented as appendages, as sex objects, as baby machines. And those women who achieve despite the terrific odds are often seen as a threat to the potential achievements of black men. Why is it not obvious that any successful effort to save black men is destined to fail if it relies on the subjugation of black women?

Kevin Powell writes about this dilemma in the current issue of *Vibe* magazine. "Somewhere in our collective mind," he writes, "black folks have managed to turn O.J. into a hero again. Because of our history in this country we immediately connect with any black person whom we perceive to be a victim of The Man. Never mind the fact that O.J. was a race-neutral athlete in his heyday, rarely going out of his way to help black causes. Never mind that O.J. repeatedly beat Nicole Brown Simpson. And never mind that for every minute of O.J. coverage there are many thousands of silent tragedies in black America." Powell concludes: "For sure O.J. will be glorified in rap songs, pimped by political leaders, his image mass-marketed in a black community near you. Then, once O.J. and his trial are out of here, we will, as the Last Poets put it, party and bullshit until there's another fallen hero to rally around."

Breaking Down the Public-Private Dichotomy

A major challenge to black scholars and activists who are interested in radical theory and practice involves the contestation of the public-private dichotomy. Racism, when we do acknowledge it, is viewed as public and political. Violence against women, on the other hand, is still seen as private and personal. And it is about time that we stop assuming that breaking down these walls is narrow feminist work, or else we all need to become feminists, women and men alike!

As Cornel West has pointed out, the notion of a private sphere is very much connected to the capitalist market, to a laissez-faire notion of what is permitted on the market. That is to say, anything goes. If we say *no* to police violence, if we say *no* to racist violence, then we have to say *no* to violence against women. This means that our notions of what counts as political need to be changed as well.

Black people have been on the forefront of radical and revolutionary movements in this country for several centuries. If we fail to address some of these critical problems, we will be left behind. Our failure thus far to incorporate into our agendas issues of gender and sexuality is, in part, a reflection of our fear of opposing capitalism. But not all of us have given up hope for revolutionary change. Not all of us accept the notion of capitalist inevitability based on the collapse of socialism. Socialism of a certain type did not work because of irreconcilable internal contradictions. Its structures have fallen. But to assume that capitalism is triumphant is to use a simplistic boxing-match paradigm. Despite its failure to build lasting democratic structures, socialism nevertheless demonstrated its superiority over capitalism on several accounts: the ability to provide free education, low-cost housing, jobs, free child care, free health care, etc. This is precisely what is needed in U.S. black communities, in other communities of color, and among poor people in general.

Harlem furnishes us with a dramatic example of the future of late capitalism and compelling evidence of the need to to reinvigorate socialist democratic theory and practice—for the sake of our sisters and brothers who otherwise will be thrown into the dungeons of the future, and indeed, for the sake of us all.

TWO

The Prison-Industrial Complex

Colorado College, Colorado Springs
May 5, 1997

I am often asked to narrate the events that led me to radical activism. *How did you become an activist? What led to your decision to
become an activist? What pivotal event was responsible for your life-
long commitment to social justice?* These are questions that I have
encountered over the years in many different contexts, questions that I have pondered over the decades. When *did* I really
become an activist? What actually led me to commit my life to
social justice work? For a long time I thought that the answers
would be as straightforward as the questions. I simply needed
to learn how to make the questions inhabit my memories.

At first I thought that the cardinal moment must have
been the 1963 bombing of the 16th Street Baptist Church in
Birmingham, Alabama, and the killing of the four girls who
were attending Sunday school. I grew up in Birmingham and
the families of Carol Robertson and Cynthia Wesley were very
close to my own family. Through my mother, we were also
connected to Denise McNair and Addie Mae Collins. Carole
Robertson's mother was my mother's dear friend; she asked my
mother to drive her to the church to pick up Carole when the
news broke that the church had been bombed. They had no
idea until they arrived at the church that Carole's life had been

taken by this act of racist terror. Carole and the other three girls were from my neighborhood; they were my sister's friends; they were girls my mother had taught in school, girls whom I knew. This egregious act of racist violence thus had a profound effect on me. So for a while I had decided that the church bombing must have been that pivotal event that explained my activism. But I later reminded myself that I had been engaged in radical activism long before the 1963 bombing. This catastrophic moment had clearly solidified my sense of what I needed to do in the world, but it was not the complete story.

After reflecting on various likely explanations and possible pivotal moments in my life, I eventually realized that I had never experienced a single epiphany that directed my life toward social activism. The answers to these questions did not contain the anticipated drama my questioners and I were seeking. The answers turned out to be quite ordinary. There had never been a dramatic moment. Rather there had been a protracted process of learning how to live with racial segregation without allowing it to fully inhabit my psyche. During my childhood years, Birmingham, Alabama, was the most segregated city in the United States. My parents made sure that all of their children recognized that racial segregation was not a permanent set of relations. They encouraged me and my siblings to be critical of the way things were, in order that we might be able to affirm our own humanity. They taught us to dedicate our lives to social transformations that would make this a better world for us all. They taught us to imagine new possibilities, new worlds, and to connect the small things one does to those possible futures.

Wherever I am, whatever I happen to be doing, I try to feel connected to futures that are only possible through struggle. So I want to begin by suggesting that whoever you are, wherever you are, whether you are a student, a teacher, a worker, a person involved in your church, an artist, there are always ways to gear your work toward progressive, radical transformation. I hope my presentation persuades you—if indeed you need persuading—that our society is in need of radical structural change.

Fear of Crime, Reality of Prisons
I have been thinking about the prison system for a very long time. In fact, my own stint in jail was directly related to my antiprison work in California during the late 1960s. I was one of many young activists who worked to free political prisoners as well as people whose prison experiences had radicalized them. We were very angry that vast numbers of people of color were being incarcerated at a time when the law-and-order rhetoric associated with then President Nixon was so clearly laden with racism. George Jackson was a young revolutionary, a self-taught and brilliant thinker and strategist, who at age 18 had been convicted of being involved in a $70 gas station robbery. Jackson was sentenced to from one year to life by the California Youth Authority, which meant that he could have been released after one year, or he could have been doomed to spend the rest of his life in prison. As it turns out, he did spend the rest of his relatively short life behind bars. He was killed twelve years after he was sentenced.

Working within movements to free political prisoners— George Jackson and the Soledad Brothers; Los Siete de La Raza; Huey Newton, Ericka Huggins, Bobby Seale, and other members of the Black Panther Party—we became aware of larger structural issues. Political repression was not only directed at political prisoners. Rather, the prison system as a whole served as an apparatus of racist and political repression, fixing its sights not only on those who were incarcerated for unambiguously political reasons, but on the majority of the in-carcerated population. The fact that virtually everyone behind bars was (and is) poor and that a disproportionate number of them were black and Latino led us to think about the more comprehensive impact of punishment on communities of color and poor communities in general. How many rich people are in prison? Perhaps a few here and there, many of whom reside in what we call country club prisons. But the vast majority of prisoners are poor people. A disproportionate number of those poor people were and continue to be people of color, people of African descent, Latinos, and Native Americans.

Some of you may know that the most likely people to go to prison in this country today are young African American men. In 1991, the Sentencing Project released a report indicating that one in four of all young black men between the ages of 18 and 24 were incarcerated. Twenty-five percent is an astonish-ing figure. That was in 1991. A few years later, the Sentencing Project released a follow-up report revealing that within three or four years, the percentage had soared to over 32 percent. In other words, approximately one-third of all young black men in this country are either in prison or directly under the super-vision and control of the criminal justice system. Something is clearly wrong.

The expansion of the criminal justice system, and the emergence of a prison-industrial complex is accompanied by an ideological campaign to persuade us once again in the late twentieth century that race is a marker of criminality. The fig-ure of the criminal is a young black man. Young black men engender fear. Black people are not impervious to this ideo-logical process. Not only white people—and others who are not black—learn how to fear black men. Black people learn how to be afraid of black youth as well.

When we speak about the representation of the young black man as criminal, this is not to deny the fact that there are some young black men who commit horrible acts of violence. But this cannot justify the wholesale criminalization of young black men. Racism, incidentally, has always relied on the conflation of the individual and the group. The fact that increasing numbers of people of color are being sent to prison has a great deal to do with the expansion of the prison system and the development of new technologies of repression. It used to be the case that the very evocation of the prison was linked to the notion of rehabilitation. It was assumed that people went to prison in order to pay their debts to society, and to learn how to become better citizens. Regardless of whether these assumptions reflected the realities of imprisonment, it is significant that the very concept of rehabilitation has become anachronistic. Incapacitation and punishment are now the unmitigated goals of imprisonment; there is not even a veneer of rehabilitation. One of the most recent developments is the super-maximum security prisons. Within these dehumanizing institutions of our democracy, people live in cells eight by sixteen feet with no fresh air, no windows, no human contact. Here in Colorado, at the federal supermax prison in Florence, prisoners have electronic escorts when they move from place to place. They are required to be in their cells for twenty-three hours a day, with one hour of exercise, but they sometimes get even less.

How can we account for these new developments? Why are we not up in arms about the soaring number of prisons and the emergence of regimes of repression that recapitulate old techniques within the context of new, computerized environments? Many of us participate in the processes that allow for the construction of ever more prisons. We vote in favor of prison bonds. We vote for three-strikes-and-you're-out laws. These are uncritical responses to the rhetoric employed by the media and by politicians who exploit the public fear of crime manufactured during the Reagan-Bush era and further deepened under Clinton. What happens if we face the current realities and ask why, in the last fifteen years or so, prisons have become increasingly necessary to our sense of security. What happens if we try to untangle the ideologies underlying this focus on crime?

We cannot deny that most of us are extremely afraid of crime. We cringe when we imagine the possibility of being the victim of a crime. It is true that we are surrounded by it, and I'm not going to suggest that it isn't real. There is indeed a lot of real crime, but it is not always committed by the people who are deemed by contemporary discourse to be the archetypical criminals. For example, there is corporate crime, oil spills and other crimes against the environment that will harm people for generations to come. But of course, those who are responsible for these far-ranging crimes are never considered to be criminals. If they are punished for their actions, they generally only pay relatively ismall fines.

If we turn to the acts of violence that flare up in our imaginations when the specter of crime is evoked, we discover that there has not been a substantial increase in crime, except—and this is extremely important—among youth. But, in general, where we have seen the most consequential rise in crime is in the media. In other words, there has been an extraordinary rise in the *representation* of crime and violence in the media—television and the movies. We're surrounded by mediated crime. We learn to fear crime in a way that does not reflect the actual threat of crime in our streets. Rather, we transfer to crime other fears for which we have no mode of expression. The message we receive from politicians and from the interminable series of crime programs on television is that we need not be afraid of unemployment, homelessness, the deterioration of conditions in poor communities; they endlessly suggest that we need not be afraid of war and the environmental degradation caused by business and military operations, but we should be afraid of crime and those who are represented as its most likely perpetrators.

Public Enemies

From my own experience, I can tell you what it is like to be treated as a public enemy. When I was a member of the Communist Party, I accepted a teaching position at UCLA, but before I had a chance to teach my first class, I was fired by the Board of Regents at the instigation of Ronald Reagan, who was the governer of California at that time. I did not know that such hatred was possible until I found myself the target of the most venomous attacks. I received many thousands of hate letters from people in California and across the country who told me to "go back to Russia." Of course I had never been to Russia, nor had I been to Africa, where some of the letters told me I should "go back." (I have since visited both parts of the world.) What I found interesting then, and what can help us to understand the contemporary racialization of fear, is the way these people so cavalierly merged my blackness and my communist-ness.

During the McCarthy era, communism was established as the enemy of the nation and came to be represented as the enemy of the "free world." During the 1950s, when membership in the CPUSA was legally criminalized, many members were forced underground and/or were sentenced to many years in prison. In 1969, when I was personally targeted by anti-communist furor, black activists in such organizations as the Black Panther Party were also singled out. As a person who represented both the communist threat and the black revolutionary threat, I became a magnet for many forms of violence. The anti-communist and racist epithets used in the hate letters I received were so terrible that I do not want to say them aloud. If we can understand how people could be led to fear communism in such a visceral way, it might help us to apprehend the ideological character of the fear of the black criminal today.

The U.S. war in Vietnam lasted as long as it did because it was fueled by a public fear of communism. The government and the media led the public to believe that the Vietnamese were their enemy, as if it were the case that the defeat of the racialized communist enemy in Vietnam would ameliorate U.S. people's lives and make them feel better about themselves. With the socialist world in collapse, other figures have now moved into the vacuum created by the fact that anti-communist rhetoric has receded. In the absence of the communist, the feared enemy has now become the criminal, the racialized criminal. The image of the new enemy is the young black or Latino man. Black women are also increasingly demonized as well. The woman of color on welfare is represented as pillaging the money earned by upstanding taxpayers. This racialized rhetoric on the welfare system helped to lead to its disestablishment. When you consider how much national political debate focused on welfare, although welfare claimed less than one percent of the budget, we see that the ideological attack on welfare mothers can tell us something about the way enemies are created.

Now that the welfare system has been disestablished and no jobs are available for women who used welfare as a safety net, how will they find work? How will they pay for child care in order to guarantee the conditions that will allow them to work? What will happen to these women, who have been made to embody the enemy of society? Many of them will seek alternative modes of survival, since they can no longer depend on welfare. Many will be lured into the drug economy or the economy in sexual services, two of the major alternatives available to people barred from the mainstream economy. This will send them straight into a jail or prison, and their presence there will justify the further expansion of the prison-industrial complex. This is a clear strategy of blaming the victim.

Since we are focuing on the creation of public enemies, we should look at the virulent attacks on immigrants. It is not accidental that as the anti-crime rhetoric and the anti-welfare rhetoric has developed, an anti-immigrant rhetoric has emerged. This anti-immigrant discourse effectively criminalizes people from other countries, especially people from the Americas and Asia, who come to the United States in order to make better lives.

Interestingly, the largest number of "illegal" immigrants come from European countries. But it is rarely assumed that a white person might be in the country illegally. Students from Britain, France, and other European countries sometimes overstay their visas, but they rarely feel threatened as do undocumented Mexican workers. Many immigrants from Europe, those who are considered to be white people, are not afraid of the U.S. immigration authorities. On the other hand, people of color who who are legally citizens or permanent residents, often fear what the INS might do to them. They know that if they forget their ID, they might be deported. They know that they have been made to embody the enemy.

In these examples of the production of public enemies, the

respective communities have already been rendered vulnerable by the impact of racism. In the public imagination they become personifications of the enemy, the racialized public enemy.

Structural Connections

The connections between the criminalization of young black people and the criminalization of immigrants are not random. In order to understand the structural connections that tie these two forms of criminalization together, we will have to consider the ways in which global capitalism has transformed the world. What we are witnessing at the close of the twentieth century is the growing power of a circuit of transnational corporations that belong to no particular nation-state, that are not expected to respect the laws of any given nation-state, and that move across borders at will in perpetual search of maximizing profits.

Let me tell you a story about my personal relationship with one of these transnational corporations—Nike. In the 1970s, when the Nike brand was created, I was just beginning to train as a recreational runner. I was really impressed by a small company in Oregon that was producing innovative running shoes. My first pair of serious running shoes were Nikes. Over the years I became so attached to Nikes that I convinced myself that I could not run without wearing them. I have run in Nike Air, Airmax, Airmax Squared. But once I learned about the conditions under which these shoes are produced, I could not in good conscience buy another pair of their running shoes. It may be true that Michael Jordan and Tiger Woods have multimillion-dollar contracts with Nike, but in Indonesia and Vietnam Nike has creating working conditions that, in many respects, resemble slavery.

Not long ago there was an investigation of the Nike factory in Ho Chi Minh City, and it was discovered that the young women who work in Nike's sweatshops there were paid less than the minimum wage in Vietnam, which is only $2.50 a day. Nike workers make $1.60 a day. Consider what you pay for Nikes and the vast differential between the price and the workers' wages. This differential is the basis for Nike's rising profits. In a report on Nike factories, Thuyen Nguyen of Vietnam Labor Watch described an incident during which fifty-six women were forced to run around the perimeter of the Ho Chi Minh factory because they were not wearing the right shoes. "One day during our two-week visit, fifty-six women workers at a Nike factory were forced to run around the factory's premise because they weren't wearing regulation shoes. Twelve people fainted during the run and were taken to the hospital. This was particularly painful to the Vietnamese because it occurred on International Women's Day, an important holiday when Vietnam honors women." This is only one of many incidents. If you read the entire report, you will be outraged to learn of the abominable treatment endured by the young women and girls who produce the shoes and the apparel we wear. The details of the report include the fact that during an eight-hour shift, workers are able to use the toilet only once, and they are prohibited from drinking water more than twice. There is sexual harrassment, inadequate health care, and excessive overtime. What was Nike's response to this report? They invited Andrew Young (another black man alongside Tiger Woods and Michael Jordan) to be their main spokesperson in connection with this investigation.

Perhaps we need we need to discuss the possibility of an organized boycott of Nike. Are there any members of the college basketball team here this evening? Basketball teams usually swear on their Nikes, don't they? I recently had a conversation with the hip hop musician Michael Franti, leader of Spearhead, who also plays basketball. He told me that he was going to try and organize the people with whom he plays basketball to stop buying Nikes. Given the global reach of corporations like Nike, we need to think about a global boycott.

Corporations move to developing countries because it is extremely profitable to pay workers $2.50 a day or less in wages. That's $2.50 a day, not $2.50 an hour, which would still be a pittance. Workers are paid more than that by McDonald's. Moreover, a direct consquence of exploiting human workers living in countries of the global South is the deindustrialization of U.S. cities. Automobile companies no longer want to pay the wages and respect the benefits demanded by the United Automobile Workers of America. In other words, the migration of corporations to the global South is in large part an attack on the organized labor movement. The question we pose to help us understand the strutural relationship between global capitalism and the prison-industrial complex has to do with the fate all of those people (and their children) who historically have worked with those corporations that have recently decided that it is more profitable to set up shop in a Third World country where they evade the demands of labor unions. These are precisely the people who end up participating in alternative economies—in the illicit drug economy—and who end up taking illicit drugs in order to alleviate the emotional pain of not being able to make a decent living.

The corporations that have migrated to Mexico, Vietnam, and other Third World countries also often end up wreaking havoc on local economies. They create cash economies that displace subsistence economies and produce artificial unemployment. Overall, the effect of capitalist corporations colonizing Third World countries is one of pauperization. These corporations create poverty as surely as they reap rapacious profits. Just as we have considered the fate of people who are left with no prospect of jobs once corporations leave U.S. cities, we can also reflect on the fate of people who can no longer live in their home countries as a direct result of the presence of capitalist corporations. When these men and women acknowledge that they have no real future in their home countries, they often look toward the United States, which is falsely represented in global public discourse as a place where any and all will thrive, as a place for a better life, as a place to put back together lives that have been torn asunder by profit-obsessed corporations.

Immigrant populations often travel along the same routes that have been carved out by migrating corporations. They simply retrace them in reverse. All they want is a chance at a decent life. But here in United States, these work-seeking people are demonized and criminalized. They are deemed responsible for unemployment and they are arrested by the INS and thrown into detention facilities that are an increasingly crucial ingredient of the prison-industrial complex. Workers flee the appalling working conditions in Vietnam, risking arrest if they have no documents. Poor black youth—and Vietnamese American youth as well—are persuaded by sophisticated Nike ads, featuring the likes of Michael Jordon and Tiger Woods—that they cannot live without Nikes. Thus they sometimes steal the money to pay for a $120 pair of Nikes. These are the processes we should describe to those who believe that the enemies of society are immigrants, welfare mothers, and prisoners.

The Prison-Industrial Complex

What these processes reveal are the economic and social conditions that have helped to produce what we call the prison-industrial complex. Prisons catch the chaos that is intensified by de-industrialization. People are left without livable futures. Jobs become unavailable because corporations close shop in the United States and move across national borders in search of ever cheaper pools of labor. Prisons and immigrant detention facilities emerge to catch those who engage in illegal acts because they are searching for better lives. And, ironically, these new prisons are represented as a secure source of employment for those who have few remaining employment opportunities.

Many of you are aware of the fact that the largest federal prison complex in the country is located not far from here in Florence, Colorado. Before the construction of the Federal Correctional Institution at Florence, local citizens held bake sales and sold T-shirts to raise $128,000 to purchase land, which they donated to the Bureau of Prisons. The Bureau accepted this land and eventually constructed a $200 million prison compound that now incarcerates more than 2,500 people. Community people banded together to attract prison construction because they assumed that the presence of a prison would boost the local economy.

Indeed, one of the most developed sectors of the contemporary construction industry is prison construction. This is where profits can be gleaned. Of course, this means that there is a demand for architects who are willing to design new prisons. There is a demand for construction materials, cell designs, and the development of new technologies. In other words, it is not possible to separate the rising punishment industry from the developing economy in the era of global capitalism. Another indication of the embeddedness of punishment in the capitalist economy is the trend toward prison privatization. Like all other capitalist corporations, private prisons run on the principle of maximizing profit. Moreover, corporations that are not directly involved in the punishment industry have begun to rely on prison labor, because the labor of women, children, and men living in developing nations can be more thoroughly exploited.

Prisons have become an integral part of the U.S. economy, which, in turn, creates profit-based pressure for the ongoing expansion of the prison business. The process is one of expanding prisons, incarcerating more people, and drawing more corporations into the punishment industry, thus creating the momentum for further expansion and larger incarcerated populations. If we do not attempt to intervene and stop this process right now, we will move into the next millennium as an increasingly incarcerated society. When I say that I am frightened by this possibility, I am speaking as a person who knows what it is like to live under conditions of incarceration. Of course, I cannot pretend to have experienced the terrors produced by supermax prisons and control units. But I can tell you how hard it was to live in conditions of solitary confinement for fifteen months. When I think back on that period of my life, I realize that I had an advantage over many people because I had spent many years of my life as a student. I was used to spending many hours at a time alone, studying. I am very serious when I say that reading and writing helped me to safeguard my sanity. Reading, writing, and yoga. But what about people who have not acquired the skills and discipline to study for hours on end? A substantial proportion of people sent to prison are functionally illiterate. How will they survive? In the years to come, to what extent will prisons create more mental disorders as they falsely claim to generate more security?

I have not painted this bleak portrait of a future prisonized society because I want you to feel apprehensive and depressed about the future. On the contrary, I want you to feel bold, courageous, and prepared to collectively challenge the prison-industrial complex. This prison-industrial complex has materialized and mushroomed because we have all learned how to forget about prisons; we push them into the background even if they're in our own neighborhoods—unless, of course, we want one because we labor under the illusion that it will solve our economic problems. We are afraid to face the realities of the prison industry even if we have relatives and friends in prison. In communities of color almost everybody knows someone who has been or still is in prison. But we have not learned how to talk about the centrality of prison in our lives. We do not integrate discussions about this institution into our daily conversations. We rarely teach about the prison system, except in specialized courses that rely on academic discourses that bolster the idea that prisons and their attendant regimes of repression are necessary institutions in a society that promises security. We have not learned how to talk about prisons as institutions that collect and hide away the people whom society treats as its refuse.

Prisons allow this society to discard people who have serious social problems rather than recognize that many of them are simply hurting themselves and are in need of help. They are simply thrown away. Because disproportionate numbers of people behind bars are people of color, structural racism enables this process. Given the histories of colonization, slavery, and other forms of racist violence, the active use of the criminal justice system to permanently discard large numbers of young people of color is quite consistent with previous modes of racist dehumanization and destruction. Let us not forget that the majority of women who have found their way into prison are incarcerated on drug-related and mostly "nonviolent" charges. Recall our discussion on the disestablishment of the welfare system. The dismantling of institutions that purportedly help human beings to survive has been accompanied by an increase in the number and intensity of repressive institutions. According to the conservative popular discourse, people who are in prison deserve to be there. They deserve to be thrown away. If poor men and women of color are incarcerated, they belong there, and everyone is absolved of the responsibility of thinking about them. Those who are relieved of the burden of thinking about people in prison are also not obligated to think about the myriad of social problems in the lives and communities of people in prison. They are not obligated to think about poverty, illiteracy, bad school systems, racism, drugs, and so on.

But those of us who do recognize the processes of criminalization that have helped to generate the prison-industrial complex should try to shed light on these issues. People who have relatives or friends in prison should not have to feel ashamed. The ideologies that support the prison system demonize those who have been touched by it, and many of us are afraid to admit that we know someone who could be the kind of person who is behind bars. But prisoners are like you, and prisoners are like me. There may be bad people in prison, but there are also good people in prison. There may be good people in the so-called free world, but there are also some very bad people who walk the streets of the free world enjoying permanent immunity.

Moreover, prisons play a central role in the process of manufacturing crime and manufacturing criminals. This is true both in a literal sense and in a more expansive ideological sense. With respect to the literal production of crime and criminals, it is obvious that the institution of the prison with its vast collection of human beings is a venue that allows for the sharing of criminal skills. I learned a great deal about "boasting" during the few weeks I lived in the jail's main population. For example, one woman boasted that she could walk out of a store with a color television set hidden between her legs. Of course TV sets in the pre-big-screen era were much smaller. The sparsity of educational and recreational activities means that she could teach the women on the corridor how to walk naturally with various objects—books and other things—between their legs. This was the main attraction. I wonder how may new careers resulted from these lessons. If you wish to reflect more deeply on the role played by the prison in the production of criminality, read Michel Foucault's *Discipline and Punish: The Birth of the Prison*.

Communications Between the Free World and the Unfree World

So what can we do? If we agree to begin by acknowledging that there is no essential difference between people in prison and people in the free world, if we begin by attempting to eradicate the shame that often accompanies revelations that we have friends and family in prison, then we can seek to create more contact between the inside and the outside, and between prison and what prisoners call the "free world." From the vantage point of prisoners, we inhabit the free world. This world certainly isn't free for many people out here, but we can, at least, take advantage of our mobility, which vastly exceeds that of people beind bars. Perhaps we can reimagine the relationship between prisoners and their allies outside as recapitulating, in part, the historical relationship between enslaved people and abolitionists. Obvious vestiges of enslavement persist within the U.S. prison system. The Thirteenth Amendment abolished slavery for all except those who have been convicted of a crime. That is why many of us have suggested that we need a modern-day abolitionist movement. Our approach to abolition involves much more than the abolition of prisons. It also involves the creation of new institutions that will effectively speak to the social problems that lead people to prison.

Just as anti-slavery abolitionism called for new schools, so anti-prison abolitionism also emphasizes educational institutions. It costs far more to send a person to prison than it does to send him or her to a college or university. Many people who are now in prison would be much better off in an institution of learning like this one than in the prisons in which they are currently incarcerated. They might even do better than some of the current students here.

What if students, faculty, and workers here thought about ways of creating lines of communication between college and university communities on the one hand and prison communities on the other? Coalitional formations that link academic communities and imprisoned communities can potentially produce great changes. People in prisons are generally considered to be people who have no agency. We often fail to recognize that prisoners are human beings who have a right to participate in transformative projects, large and small. In this context I will share my own experiences of creating productive traffic between the prison and the university. Some years ago I taught a class on incarcerated women in the Women's Studies Department at San Francisco State University. I took a number of students from the San Francisco State class to the San Francisco County jail, where I also taught a class. The assumption—both from the students and the prisoners—was that the students would assist me to teach the prisoners. However, I decided to position the prisoners as teachers, at least in the beginning. They taught the students about life in jail, what went on there, what the major problems were, and they got to choose how the students, those in posession of formal learning, could effectively assist the prisoners. This reversal of assumed hierarchies of knowledge created a radical and exciting learning environment. Moroever, at the conclusion of the course, most of the students who had participated in the jail visits sought ways to continue their work on issues helping imprisoned people.

Students, teachers, community activists, artists, and cultural workers can gain entrance into jails and prisons. By teaching classes, and especially by querying the usual hierarchies, the inside-outside traffic can be transformative. Since the people who are inside are not allowed out, the people who are outside need to knock on the gates of the nation's prisons and jails. This would be a small step forward. This would be a beginning challenge to the ideological prison that has silenced protest against the prison-industrial complex.

Finally, I want to situate these reflections on the prison-industrial complex within a larger frame, one that includes the continued assault against affirmative action and rising political conservatism. Visiting Colorado Springs, I cannot forget that the Focus on the Family complex is also headquartered here. What is so dangerous about this organization is its ideological representation of the family. According to their conservative views, the family on which they are focusing is a patriarchal nuclear family: The woman's role is to be a good wife and mother, and the father's role is to be the provider and the head of the family. This means that the single mother and her children (especially if they are black or Latina/o, and especially if the mother is in prison) don't really count as a family. This particular construction of the family, is also heterosexist. Gays and lesbians can never have "real" families, according to the Focus on the Family people, because the rest of us have remained relatively silent. Therefore I urge every single one of you who have come out to participate in this community-building gathering to reflect deeply and seriously about what you can each do help create livable futures for us all.

THREE

Race, Crime, and Punishment

University of Wisconsin, Madison
November 16, 1999

I want to talk about a number of interrelated issues I have been following for most of my life: prisoners' rights, the urgent but generally unacknowledged problems facing women in prison, and the complex ways in which racism anchors punishment practices in the United States. Along with many other individuals associated with the Critical Resistance movement, I am engaged in a long-term anti-racist project of creating a broad mass movement against the prison-industrial complex. We are attempting to encourage people everywhere—on the campus, in the workplace, in the prison itself—to think critically about the emergence of an ever expanding, ever more repressive prison system, and about the economic, political, and ideological stakes in the punishment industry that have created a set of relations that recapitulate the development of the military-industrial complex. This prison-industrial complex is not confined to the United States and cannot be considered within a purely local context. As capitalism itself has become more globalized, so have prison industries and technologies become globalized. One of the most alarming developments associated with the global prison-industrial complex is the marketing of the new super-maximum security prisons—supermaxes—by U.S. companies in Europe, Africa, and elsewhere in the world.

Considering the spectrum of public punishment, the most repressive and dehumanizing penalty to impose is death. That people continue to be put to death under the auspices of state governments in the United States today is a resounding comment on how far behind much of the world we are in regard to modern notions of human rights, the sanctity of life, and the purpose of punishment and rehabilitation. If we wish to understand the circumstances that enabled the emergence of a prison-industrial complex, it's necessarily expanding population of prisoners, and its profitable technologies, we can begin by breaking the silence about the veritable assembly line of death that currently extends across the country. The collective reluctance to critically engage with the death penalty finds its parallel in the reluctance to develop a public conversation about punishment generally and to think about what it means to live in a country in which almost two million people are behind bars, and almost five million are directly under the control of the criminal justice system. What does it mean to claim that the United States of America is a democratic society, but that this democracy relies fundamentally on carceral institutions, as it also relies on the death penalty? Prisons are totalitarian institutions, just as the death penalty is an obsolete and totalitarian form of punishment.

Here in Wisconsin, you can claim that your state has been able to conduct its criminal justice work without resorting to capital punishment for almost 150 years. Wisconsin abolished the death penalty in 1851 and is one of twelve abolitionist states. At this time, capital punishment is illegal in Hawaii, Alaska, Iowa, Maine, Massachusetts, Michigan, Minnesota,

North Dakota, Rhode Island, Vermont, West Virginia, Wisconsin, and the District of Columbia.

Today there are more than 3,500 people on death row in the United States. In California 536 prisoners live on death row, more people than were on death row in the entire country in 1969. Texas can claim the second-highest number of prisoners on death row as well as a presidential candidate who brazenly celebrates this machinery of death. Florida is third, with 390 people currently waiting for society to kill them. The fourth-largest death-row population can be found in Pennsylvania, where there are approximately 225 people currently on death row. The most well-known inhabitant of Pennsylvania's death house is Mumia Abu-Jamal, who is one of our most important public intellectuals today. My most recent visit with Mumia inspired me to think more urgently about our public acceptance of capital punishment and our failure to fully engage with the idea that in this putatively democratic society, we collectively give the state permission to kill us. Currently, approximately thirty-five people have received their execution dates. Several days ago, a man by the name of Leroy Joseph Drayton was executed in South Carolina.

The further normalization of capital punishment occurs in insidious ways. The Texas case that resulted from the lynching last year of a U.S. citizen, James Byrd, was particularly disturbing. Three white men were convicted of intentionally chaining Byrd to a pickup truck and dragging him to his death. When the first defendant was found guilty and sentenced to death, *Jet* magazine published a photograph of a white policeman embracing a black policeman, celebrating, it seems, the road to equality paved by execution and death. We are in very difficult straits if the measure of equality has become the right to execute white people for killing people of color. Where, indeed, are we headed, if people who consider themselves anti-racist can be seduced in this way to join the ranks of those who support capital punishment?

Last May I attended a vigil outside San Quentin prison. That night, the State of California killed a fifty-year-old black man by the name of Manny Babbitt was executed that night. Ironically, his execution date coincided with his fiftieth birthday. So among all of the people who had gathered for the vigil, his family was there simultaneously celebrating his birthday and witnessing his death. Manny Babbitt had committed a terrible act of violence. Babbitt's attorneys argued that when he killed a 78-year-old woman, he was in the throes of a post-traumatic stress episode related to his experiences in Vietnam, where he had been involved in one of the war's bloodiest battles. In Vietnam, he killed, was wounded, was mistaken for dead, and regained consciousness in a helicopter where he had been thrown on a pile of corpses. Ironically, Babbitt received a Purple Heart that the U.S. government delivered to him on death row at San Quentin, and after he was executed he was buried with full military honors. This man, whom the state taught to kill so efficiently, returned from Vietnam and killed again, and killed terribly. And in the end, the state killed him as well. This case reveals many of the contradictions swirling around the death penalty. Manny Babbitt was 50 years old. In California there is an initiative currently supported by our new Democratic governor, Gray Davis—the Juvenile Criminal Justice Initiative—that proposes to *lower* the age at which a person can receive the death penalty so that ever younger people will be executed at San Quentin in the future.

I urge you to really think seriously about this machinery of death. I urge you to reflect on the reasons why the United States of America is the only country in the industrialized world that routinely and cavalierly puts civilians to death. Numerous historical ironies can be discovered in the persistence of capital punishment, but none so revealing as the fact that the institution of the prison was introduced during the era of the rise of democracy precisely as an alternative to corporal and capital punishment. Imprisonment as punishment, with all its own problems and contradictions, was supposed to displace and supplant capital punishment.

The Prison and Democracy

Historically, the penitentiary emerged around the same time as the idea of a society in which citizens are defined as rights-bearing subjects. In the late 1700s, capital punishment was viewed as obsolete and barbaric, as obsolete, indeed, as the monarchy. The penitentiary was introduced as a humane alternative to corporal punishment and the infliction of death. The new, alternative punishment consisted of depriving people of their rights and their liberties. The deprivation of liberty was the essential nature of the punishment itself. Such a conception of punishment was only possible in a society that recognized its citizens as rights-bearing subjects. It was only possible in a society whose citizens were supposed to be free. The first penitentiaries were considered to be progressive, because they were supposed to be places where people who had committed crimes were deprived of their freedom so that they could repent and transform themselves. While historical penitentiaries were praised because they were putative alternatives to corporal punishment, they were the site of an enormous amount of suffering—mental and emotional, if not physical.

The infliction of imprisonment was thought to be humane and democratic, especially because it replaced corporal and capital punishment. It is interesting that the notion of punishment as violence inflicted on the body has insinuated itself back into popular penological discourses and practices. Many have been led to believe that not only should people be sent to prison, but while they are there they should be treated repressively, and that they should lose human rights—like the right to get an education, to recreation sports—that prisoners have historically possessed. It is possible to trace this pattern of mounting repression within the prison system by looking at the differences between mid- and late-twentieth-century women's prisons. In California, for example, what used to be the world's largest prison for women, California Institution for Women, was originally based on the domestic model associated with the reformatory movement. Just as women were considered second-class citizens (who did not enjoy many of the rights allocated to men), the reformatory role of the women's prison was focused on turning female criminals into good wives and mothers.

Last month Ted Koppel's *Nightline* was devoted to a six-episode series inside what is now the largest prison for women in the world, Valley State Prison, located in Chowchilla, California. "Valley State" is a strange name for a prison, because it sounds like the name a college. After all there is Mississippi Valley State University, Grand Valley State University, Saginaw Valley State University, and many others. From the exterior, this women's prison looks no different from the most repressive maximum-security men's prisons. While many issues were raised during Koppel's weeklong stay inside the prison, the most alarming problems revolved around health care. As Koppel revealed through his interview, many of the women are afraid to see the prison doctor, because they dreaded the numerous and unnecessary gynecological examinations imposed by the staff. After hearing many of the women talk about going to see the doctor for a headache or a cold and being given a pelvic exam, Ted Koppel asked the chief medical officer at Valley State whether this was true. The chief medical officer responded by saying on camera: "This is the only male touch that most of these women get. Many of them enjoy it."

Before the series was edited, Ted Koppel turned over the tapes to local media in Chowchilla. Consequently, the interview was broadcast on the news, and within a short period of time the head of the California Department of Corrections announced that the chief medical officer had been relieved of his position. She pointed out that he would continue to be employed by the Department of Corrections in California, but is no longer in charge of medical care at the largest women's prison in the world. Moreover, it was announced, he would never again be allowed direct contact with women patients in the prison system. While this was a small victory, we cannot avoid asking questions about the conditions within women's prisons that promoted such attitudes and overt sexual abuse under the guise of medical treatment.

Two summers ago, Radhika Coomaraswamy, the United Nations Special Rapporteur on Violence Against Women, visited women's prisons all over the United States. She attempted to visit Valley State, but the prison authorities refused to approve her visit. What does it mean to live in a democracy where there are closed institutions that engage in repressive and totalitarian practices? Many of these practices are justified by demonizing those who live within these institutions. But regardless of what anyone has done, she or he does not deserve to be objectified and subjected to sexual abuse. Moreover, there is a broad range of people in prison. Some have done horrible things. Some may need to be isolated from society for purposes of treatment. But on the other hand, there are those who have committed small, nonviolent acts. There are those in prison on welfare fraud. There are those who are in prison because they have serious problems with drugs. The majority of women prisoners and many men prisoners have faced drug-related charges. Yet we tend to think about the "prisoner" in terms that fail to allow distinctions between the almost two million individuals who live in these institutions today. In the popular imagination, there is a homogeneous conception of the prisoner.

Many of us imagine the prisoner as a black person. And, of course, it is true that black people constitute almost half of the prison population, not just here in Wisconsin, but all over the country. Of course, in Wisconsin you have a particularly egregious situation because black people only constitute 4 or 5 percent of the state's population and about 50 percent of the imprisoned population. Our criminal justice system sends increasing numbers of people to prison by first robbing them of housing, health care, education, and welfare, and then punishing them when they participate in underground economies. What should we think about a system that will, on the one hand, sacrifice social services, human compassion, housing and decent schools, mental health care and jobs, while on the other hand developing an ever larger and ever more profitable prison system that subjects ever larger numbers of people to daily regimes of coercion and abuse? The violent regimes inside prisons are located on a continuum of repression that includes state-sanctioned killing of civilians.

Race, Class, and Capital Punishment
I wish I could say that the only major problem facing us in this country is the obsolescence of the death penalty. I wish I could reasonably say that we simply need a more effective anti–death

penalty campaign and that once we manage to abolish capital punishment, we will have done important work to safeguard democracy and build a radically democratic future. If it is true that capital punishment needs to be understood in relation to the prison-industrial complex, both require us to tackle the broader issues of racism and class bias. Thirty-five percent of people who have been executed since 1976 were black. Forty-three percent of today's death-row inmates are black. Eight percent are Latino. Forty-six percent are white. Although 50 percent of all murder victims are white, 84 percent of the victims of those who are sentenced to death are white. Why are some people sentenced to death and others are not?

If you look at the population of death row prisoners, you see that almost every single person there is poor. Generally speaking, white people on death row are usually economically poor. In other words, race and class together create the social context that helps to determine who will be sent to the death house and whose life will be saved. So what does it mean to assent to a system of punishment in which one's economic status may very well determine whether one gets to live or die?

There is a correlation between the rising use of capital punishment and the growing problem of police brutality, as evidenced by the recent police murder of Amadou Diallo. We are all familiar with the criminalization of race embedded in racial profiling. The same people who sit on the country's death row are those who are subject to the crimes of driving while black, driving while brown. The racial profiling perpetrated in police departments all over the country is simply one indication of the degree to which the practices of the police are deeply informed by racism.

Racism Toward Refugees and Immigrants

Coercive treatment of refugees and immigrants by the Immigration and Naturalization Services (INS) is interrelated with capital punishment, the prison-industrial complex, and police violence. The INS now has the largest group of armed federal agents in the country. There are more armed INS agents, for example, than there are armed FBI agents. And why has immigration emerged as such a major problem? It cannot be denied that immigration is on the rise. In many cases, however, people are compelled to leave their home countries because U.S. corporations have economically undermined local economies through "free trade" agreements, structural adjustment, and the influence of such international financial institutions as the World Bank and the International Monetary Fund.

Rather than characterize "immigration" as the source of the current crisis, it is more accurate to say that it is the *homelessness* of global capital that is responsible for so many of the problems people are experiencing throughout the world. Many transnational corporations that used to be required to comply with a modicum of rules and regulations in the nation-states where they are headquartered have found ways to evade prohibitions against cruel, dehumanizing, and exploitative labor practices. They are now free to do virtually anything in the name of maximizing profits. Fifty percent of all of the garments purchased in the United State are made abroad by women and girls in Asia and Latin America. Many immigrant women from those regions who come to this country hoping to find work do so because they can no longer make a living in their home countries. Their native economies have been dislocated by global corporations. But what do they find here in the United States? More sweatshops. In fact, even those companies that claim that their products are manufactured in the United

States frequently rely on sweatshops that pay women and girls sub-minimum wage.

A few years ago, the Asian Immigrant Women Advocates conducted a successful campaign against Jessica McClintock, whose company was selling prom dresses for approximately $175 each, while contracting sweatshops that paid Asian women who do not speak English only $5 per dress to make them. Big corporations like Jessica McClintock Inc. rarely engage directly with sweatshop labor. They work through subcontractors—in the case of McClintock, it was Lucky Sewing Company. When the subcontractor declared bankruptcy and closed down without even paying the women the paltry $5 per dress for the work they had done, the women sued Jessica McClintock. The amazing boycott that ensued taught many young women that to dance in Jessica McClintock dresses on their prom nights meant that they were literally wearing the exploitation of Asian immigrant women on their bodies. Those who are undocumented may be corralled in detention facilities, some of which are privately run for profit, and others of which are directly patrolled by armed INS agents. These armed figures play a major role within the prison-industrial complex.

Drugs

When we speak of the prison-industrial complex, rather than the prison system more simply, we refer to the set of economic and political relations in which the system of punishment has become embedded. Punishment has developed into an important sector of the U.S. economy. Last May, shortly after I attended the vigil for Manny Babbitt at San Quentin prison, I visited a women's prison in Australia. I have visited women's prisons in Brazil, the Netherlands, and Cuba, and what strikes me is the degree to which the patterns of racialization appear to be so similar. In Australia, who did I see in prison? I saw young Aboriginal women addicted to heroin. No one asks, why and how they *became heroin addicts*. No one asks why poor Aboriginal people in Australia and poor black and Latino people in the United States are so attracted to consciousness-altering substances.

What would it mean to think about the issues of drugs more broadly, so as to simultaneously reflect on illicit and legal psychotropic drugs? We might discover a connection between the ways in which the pharmaceutical companies present their drugs as panaceas, particularly the new generation of psychotropic drugs that includes Paxil, Zoloft, and Prozac. It may well be the case that those substances have helped many people, but when they are represented as the solution to complicated psychological problems, when they are represented as miracle remedies, the reverberations of these advertisements also reach people who cannot afford doctors who will give them Prozac prescriptions. Media rhetoric, especially in advertisements, affects those who may have no legal avenue to drugs, but for whom illegal markets are always readily available. Some people find themselves in prison for using psychotropic drugs, while others are congratulated. Class and race mark this difference.

Imagining New Geographical and Social Landscapes

Why do we in this country find it so difficult to imagine a society in which prisons are not such a prominent feature of the geographical and social landscape? Our impoverished popular imagination is responsible for the lack of or sparsity of conversations on minimizing prisons and emphasizing *de*carceration as opposed to increased *in*carceration. Particularly since resources that could fund services designed to help prevent people from engaging in the behavior that leads to prison are being used instead to build and operate prisons. Precisely the resources we need in order to prevent people from going to prison are being devoured by the prison system. This means that the prison reproduces the conditions of its own expansion, creating a syndrome of self-perpetuation.

The international campaign against capital punishment has resulted in the abolition of the death penalty in two-thirds of the countries in the world. Since 1976, countries like Portugal, Denmark, the Netherlands, New Zealand, and South Africa have become abolitionist. As I pointed out earlier, Wisconsin is one of only thirteen abolitionist states, and if we include Washington, D.C., there are fourteen. Most of you are aware of the fact that there are now campaigns all over the country to comprehensively abolish the death penalty. But are you also aware of similar campaigns to abolish prisons? How many of you have heard of prison abolitionism? Unfortunately, only a handful. What does it mean to embrace a strategy of prison abolitionism at the same time that we call for the abolition of the death penalty, especially since imprisonment is traditionally posed as the logical and humane alternative to capital punishment?

What is a crime? How do you define crime? The fundamental legal definition of crime is an action in violation of the law. Wherever you have broken the law you have committed a crime. People generally refer to crimes as felonies, rather than misdemeanors or traffic violations. However, people break the law all the time. When you run a stop sign, for example, you break the law. Scholars who have researched the extent to which people break the law and actually commit felonies have discovered that many more people have committed crimes than ever go to prison. The question is, *what determines who has to pay for those crimes?* Why is it that one person who steals a slice of pizza—this is a famous case in L.A.—ends up being sentenced to twenty-five years under the three-strikes provision, while someone who commits the same act does not get arrested. Race, class, gender are all facts that help to determine who actually gets punished and how. The point is that punishment is not a logical consequence of crime. Punishment does not always follow crime, and you might also argue that factors other than crime play a prominent role in dictating who gets punished and who does not. This means that we can potentially develop a more compelling analysis of the prison-industrial complex if we disarticulate crime and punishment from one another. The effort to abolish prisons focuses our attention on making the world livable for all people, regardless of economic status or racial background; it focuses energy on helping, rather than harming, one another.

When the prison was first proposed as an alternative to corporal and capital punishment, its advocates argued passionately that prisons could reform, rehabilitate, prepare people to be better citizens, and give them an opportunity to reflect purposefully on their lives and to establish a relationship with God. This is why it was called a *penitentiary*. It was a place for *penitence*. Because rehabilitation was the very essence of this form of social response to crime when it was historically introduced, it would seem that acknowledgment of the failure of rehabilitation would lead to discussions about new ways of addressing crime. Today, no one ever expects people who go to prison to come out reformed. In fact, many come out in much worse condition than when they entered.

Criminologists are increasingly using the term "incapacitate." Prisons are designed to incapacitate. The language has clear resonances with the death penalty. Especially now with the three-strikes laws and mandatory minimums, prisons engage in long-term incapacitation of living beings while the death penalty—capital punishment—permanently incapacitates by killing.

How did we allow this to happen? Have you ever looked at a prison and imagined what was happening on the other side of those walls? Have you ever looked at the razor wire and imagined what it might be like to live under those repressive conditions? Has it ever occurred to you that people just like you are in prison, people who may have made one mistake and never had the opportunity to get themselves back on the right track? Instead, they were simply thrown away, treated as garbage, as detritus. Incapacitation of people in prisons is a living death that allows us to understand the persistence of the permanent incapacitation of capital punishment. Abolition—of capital punishment and of prisons—should be conceived of as innovative and humanizing alternatives to incapacitation. We can learn from the failures of anti-slavery abolition how to more effectively conceptualize the abolition of incapacitation by the death penalty and the prison. If the repressive institution is only abolished negatively, without replacing it with institutions promoting substantive freedoms, then that repression will persist, as the legacy of enslavement persists today.

Thus, we need schools—schools that don't look like and feel like prisons. One of the reasons many young poor kids end up in prison is that there is a seamless transition from their schools to juvenile hall to prison. As schoolchildren they are already treated like prisoners. When the message they receive in school is that they live in the world as objects of surveillance and discipline, and that security guards are more important and powerful than teachers, they are clearly learning how to be prisoners. We also need mental health care for people who cannot afford to go to expensive clinics. Jails and prisons have almost become like human landfills—places where society discards poor people who have serious emotional and mental disorders. We need drug programs. Poor people who want to deal with drug addiction have nowhere to go. There is no direct path from the streets to a drug rehabilitation center. In general, the abolition of prisons involves the dismantling of old institutions and the creation of new ones.

Thus we consider affirmative action an important dimension of a radical abolitionist approach to prisons and society. It's not accidental that those states that have abolished affirmative action have the largest prison populations in the country. In California, a black man is five times more likely to be found in a prison cell than in one of the classrooms of California's public colleges and universities. You here at the University of Wisconsin attend a public university that should be much more welcoming to prisoners and former prisoners than it is at present. At the very least, you can begin to apply some of the critical skills you are acquiring here to imagine and advocate for new geographical and social landscapes where state-inflicted death and prison incapacitation are memories of a distant past.

FOUR

Race, Power, and Prisons Since 9/11

Metro State College, Denver
March 1, 2002

When the figure of Osama bin Laden began to take shape in the public imagination as the epitome of evil, the general response was an all-embracing collective fear. In calling attention to the ideological dimension of the "war on terror," I do not mean to minimize the enormous loss of human life and the profound suffering generated by the attacks of 9/11. But I do want to look at the political strategy behind the moral panic which focuses on the figure of bin Laden. This strategy resonates with the McCarthy-era agenda of creating a moral panic in order to combat communism. It also resonates with the rhetorical justifications of over-incarceration. During the McCarthy era, communists were represented as the very embodiment of evil. Since the mid-1980s, criminals have been portrayed as the face of evil. Now we are witnessing the use of a similar political strategy to justify a far-reaching war on terrorism. Philosophically, the evocation of "evil" requires an attendant, implicit conception of "good." Evil always requires its opposite.

In the case of communism, its opposite, the embodiment

of good, has been capitalism. In the case of the criminal, with its subterranean racialization, the embodiment of good is the upstanding, middle-class, white citizen. When Osama bin Laden becomes the personification of evil, who represents its twin force of good? Before September 11, 2001, it would have been impossible to imagine George W. Bush as the avatar of righteousness. However, the current moral panic is constructed so as to position Bush as the national savior who confronts Osama bin Laden, the quintessential enemy. In the aftermath of 9/11, how quickly people seemed to forget that a significant number of us were not even persuaded that George Bush was the legitimate, elected president of the United States of America. We cannot forget that before 9/11, anti-prison activists had pointed out that the large-scale disenfranchisement of prisoners and former prisoners enabled Bush's rise to power. Had a small fraction of the 400,000 black men who were barred from voting in the contested state of Florida (because they were either felons or former felons) been able to vote, Bush would not have even emerged as a serious contender.

The current climate of fear has engendered an extremely masculinist form of nationalism that militates against the sense of democracy required for masses of people to stand up for civil liberties, to advocate for the rights of immigrants, and to speak out against the racial profiling of Arabs, Muslims, Middle Easterners, and South Asians. One month after the September 11 attacks, the *New York Times* published an article based on interviews with travelers who described what they would do if a hijacker attempted to take over a plane in which they were passengers. One man said that all the male passengers should stand up and fight. "It's a sorry man that would sit still during a hijacking now. I think the American citizenry as a whole, especially males, are pretty pumped about this now."[2] As an afterthought, he also included women in his hypothetical scenario, suggesting that they might "grab a leg and bite pretty hard." I urge you to think about the masculinist, heterosexist frame within which the nation is represented in this moment of crisis. The crisis allows us to understand how the nation always constitutes itself through exclusion. It allows us to understand how the very process of embracing previously marginalized communities—black people, Latinos, and some Asian-Americans, for example—leads to the exclusions of South Asians, Middle Easterners, Arabs, and Muslims.

Nationalism has never been without its dangers. Nationalism creates narrow perimeters around community, and processes of exclusion and prohibition are at its very core. Militaristic mobilizations defend the nation from its enemies, thus reinforcing exclusionary hierarchies based on gender and sexuality. Recognizing the pitfalls of nationalism should lead us to reflect on community formations that extend beyond the borders of the nation. In the immediate aftermath of September 11, when people were grieving, rethinking their lives, contemplating what is important and what might not be, many individuals were motivated to get in touch with their family and friends. Regardless of whether we had relatives and friends who died in the attacks, we all instinctively felt the need for community. Given the outpouring of condolences from all over the planet, this tragedy could have served as an occasion to reach out and create community with people in other regions of the world. Why didn't we think about building solidarity with people in Central Asia? In Africa? People everywhere were shaken up by the attacks on the World Trade Center and the Pentagon. Why were so many people within the United States persuaded that the nation had to close down and behave like a fortress under siege? Would it not have made more sense to reach out, expand, and build solidarity than to close oneself up in the house of the nation, pull out all the guns, and blast anyone who approaches?

The USA PATRIOT Act

The repressive provisions of the USA PATRIOT Act for deportation, detention, and surveillance and its deliberate curtailment of civil liberties will be extremely difficult to reverse in the months and years to come. Can you recall any serious discussions prior to the passage of this bill either in Congress or in the larger public sphere? At the moment, there are thousands of immigrants in detention centers. During the month of November, the government decided to withhold all of the statistical information about people who were being detained in INS detention centers. In some cases the only people who are aware of FBI and INS arrests are probably the friends and families of people who are often arbitrarily removed from their workplaces and their homes. Under these conditions, can we in good conscience claim that we live in a democracy? This word is repeatedly invoked to justify its own contradictions, especially when it comes from the mouth of George W. Bush.

The sinister parallels to the McCarthy era are especially apparent to me, given my own childhood encounters with the FBI. My parents had friends who were members of the Communist Party, and some of them were driven underground during the 1950s. As a result, members of my family were often followed by FBI agents. At the very young age of 5, I learned how to identify FBI agents and how not to divulge any information to them. My parents' friends' only crimes were that they believed in socialism. Because of the moral panic that proclaimed communists to be enemies of the state, countless numbers of institutions were purged of communists, their allies, and people who simply believed in democracy.

Joseph McCarthy and his conservative political backers were not the only people responsible for the anti-communist purges in academia, the labor movement, and Hollywood. Liberals were also responsible. These were the people who were afraid, those who thought that they might be associated with communism if they failed to vigorously speak out against it. Do you see the point? Many people who identified with the left assented—some simply by their silence—to the campaign to eradicate progressive ideas in the major institutions of our country.

Those of us who have been active in the anti-prison movement for the last decade or so have noticed a striking resemblance between the representation of the terrorist and the representation of the criminal. The public was already prepared for the mobilization of nationalist emotions based on the fear of a racialized enemy. This had already occurred in connection with the so-called war on crime and, indeed, had enabled the emergence of a vast prison-industrial complex that not only promoted the popular ideological assumptions that safety and security were a function of the imprisonment of vast numbers of people of color, but also, in the process, criminalized undocumented immigrants. And the expansion of the INS as an apparatus of policing and imprisonment was, as we can now see, a portentous rehearsal for the present moment.

The more than two million people in U.S. prisons, the new modes of imprisonment like super-maximum security facilities, new industries that now market prisons and prison-related products and services, the private companies that run prisons for profit around the world—all these can now be recognized as elements of a scaffolding for global repression. Prisons in the United States now serve as a global model of punishment. At this very moment in Turkey, prisoners are dying as a consequence of a protracted hunger strike, organized to protest the imposition of U.S.-style prisons with their individual, solitary cells. Moreover, South Africa, our latest hope for racial, gender, and sexual justice, can also unfortunately claim a super maximum-security prison run by the Wackenhut Corrections Corporation, a U.S.-based private prison company. These are some of the connections that demand our attention if we wish to understand the way things are going.

Things are never as simple as they appear to be. It is incumbent on us to think, to question, to be critical, and to recognize that if we do not interrogate that which we most take for granted, if we are not willing to question the anchoring ground of our ideas, opinions, and attitudes, then we will never move forward. The xenophobia that anchors the current war against terrorism is very much related to the centuries-long history of racism in U.S. popular discourse. In the early 1990s, it was claimed that racism was rapidly becoming obsolete in the United States, and that we did not need affirmative action programs any longer because African Americans, Latinos, and women of all racial backgrounds were well on the road to equality. A level playing field had been achieved. Ward Connelly, the black member of the Board of Regents of the University of California, emerged as the figurehead for this anti–affirmative action campaign, which was unfortunately successful in California—both at the level of the university and in the larger context of the state.

In California, a black man is five times more likely to be found in a prison cell than in a college classroom. We might ask, what kind of affirmative action is this? It appears to be a reversal of the original goals of affirmative action. Reverse affirmative action. But in order not to appear as if we have paraphrased the notion of "reverse racism," we can formulate this dilemma differently: In California, evidence of the most consistent affirmative action programs can actually be found in prison. An implicit affirmative action strategy has resulted in the racialization of the prison population as Latino and black. The majority of people in California prisons are Latinos. If we consider jails, as well as state and federal prisons all over the country, we discover that the prison population is two-thirds people of color. Women constitute the fastest-growing sector of the imprisoned population, and among women prisoners, women of color constitute the fastest-growing sector. Race is clearly a determining factor when it is a question of who goes to prison and who does not. It would be instructive to look inside the many prisons—both public and private, both state and federal—for which your state is known. In the small town of Florence, Colorado, whose population is slightly more than 3,500, there are four federal prisons, including the United States Penitentiary Administrative Maximum Facility, the notorious supermax. The last time I was in Colorado, I spent the day in Florence and still have vivid memories of its nightmarish prisonscape.

I have spoken about the dismantling of affirmative action programs in California, while surreptitious affirmative action strategies guarantee that the state's prisons are filled to capacity with black and Latino men and women. Interestingly, an unspoken affirmative action program seems to be at work in the hiring practices at the upper levels of the prison hierarchy. There is a conscious effort to place women of color in positions of authority. A Latina, for example, is the warden of one of the state's major, maximum-security men's prisons. You might call this the Condoleezza Rice syndrome. The point I am making is that we have to complicate our analyses now. We cannot rely on simple categories, or assume that just because a person is black or Latino/a that they are not organizers and agents of racist strategies.

Women in the leadership hierarchies of women's prisons who identify as feminists sometimes end up creating far more difficult conditions for women prisoners. A feminist warden (author of *The Warden Wore Pink*) insists that women should be treated no differently than men; women prisoners should be equal to men prisoners. Her rather simplistic argument is that when men try to escape, there is no warning shot before sharpshooters aim at them. Therefore, in order for equality to prevail, no warning shot should be fired for women. At this Michigan women's prison—I kid you not—there was a serious debate about whether women deserved to be shot at without warning, which would render them equal to the male prisoners. Discussions about the number of weapons in women's as compared to men's prisons have revealed the superficiality of those ideas about gender equality that are based on simply achieving parity with men. At this time, the trend is to make women's prisons architecturally the same as men's prisons. This presumptive equality is grounded in violence—women's prisons are rendered equal to men's by making them equally punitive, equally dehumanizing.

Racism and Immigration
In 1958, Paul Robeson wrote in his eloquent book, *Here I Stand*: "Those who tell the world that racism in American life is merely a fading hangover from the past, and is largely limited to one section of our country, cannot explain away the infamous Walter McCarran Immigration Act passed by Congress since the war. No decree of Nazi Germany was more fully racist than

this American law, which in the words of Senator Lehmann was based on the same discredited racial theories from which Adolf Hitler developed the infamous Nuremberg Laws. Look at how our immigration quotas are allotted. From Ireland's three million people, 17,000 people may come each year. But from India, with her 400 million, the quota is 100. Usually we Negroes do not think much about immigration laws, because we have been here for centuries. But in our midst there are many from the West Indies, and their talents and vitality have been important to our communities far beyond their numbers. Under the Walter McCarran act, with all of its provisions to reduce non-Nordic immigration, the number of Negroes who can come from the Caribbean or anywhere else has been drastically cut down."

The questions Paul Robeson raised in the throes of the McCarthy period about the way racism influences immigration policy are even more pertinent today. But more than forty years later, our conceptualizations of racism should reflect our awareness that it is always informed by and crosshatched with class bias, patriarchy, homophobia, etc. In other words, racism is never a set of strategies that exist by themselves. Moreover, racism changes and mutates over time. It does not remain the same while historical circumstances change. Those who campaign against affirmative action assume that because certain overt legal forms of racial discrimination have been defeated, racism itself has been overcome. However, because racism hides in the structures of our society, in the educational system, the prison system, the health care system, etc., it can do more damage than ever without provoking the kind of resistance that led to the end of racial segregation.

One of the crucial challenges confronting us today is to understand the deeply complicated character of racism in the aftermath of 9/11—racism not only as it is rooted in the enslavement of people of African descent and in the colonization of indigenous people, but also racism as it is inflicted on new immigrants. This means that it is not acceptable for black people to assume that it is all right to engage in racial profiling, as long as this profiling is not directed at black communities. Racial profiling is unjust, whoever the target. Today, more than ever, anti-racist solidarity movements must emphasize struggles in defense of immigrant rights and the importance of global, transnational, international perspectives. People who live in this country come from all over the globe. As a matter of fact, only Native Americans can claim that they are the original inhabitants of this land. Native people have created a global indigenous network that includes people from all over the Americas, Australia, Torres Strait Island, and New Zealand.

In today's era of global capitalism, resistance to racism can only be effective if it is anchored in global communities of struggle. Our challenge today is to build secure bridges that link anti-racist movements, prison abolitionist campaigns, and immigrant rights movements. Imagine the life conditions of a young girl in Mexico or Korea who works on the global assembly line making athletic shoes for which she receives a couple of dollars per pair, but that sell here for more than $100. The transnational athletic shoe corporation markets these shoes intensively in poor U.S. communities of color. Imagine that this girl's family travels to the United States because their own country has been so dislocated by capitalist corporations that they can no longer survive. Because they travel here without papers and are unable to elude the authorities, they are charged with being illegal immigrants and locked up in a prison where a young black or Latino person has been sent, perhaps even for having stolen the shoes made by this immigrant girl. This might be a fictitious scenario, but the connections it emphasizes are real. Because these are very real connections, our resistance must manifest an awareness of the interrelatedness of these issues. I urge all of you to think deeply about your potential contributions as individuals and collectively to radical and global communities of resistance.

Questions from the Audience

We've been working to abolish mandatory minimum sentencing. What strategies can we use?

Keep doing this very important work against mandatory minimums, truth-in-sentencing laws, and three-strikes laws, but at the same time encourage people to broaden the framework of their analysis. A myopic focus on one particular issue can sometimes lead to the very opposite of what one wants to achieve. In the late 1960s, an important campaign emerged against the indeterminate prison sentence, the opposite of mandatory minimums. One of the most dramatic examples in California was the case of George Jackson, who had been sent to prison as a youth for being involved in robbery that netted $70. His sentence was "one year to life." Such indeterminate sentences gave prison authorities and parole boards absolute control over the fate of prisoners. We called for an end to these repressive practices and eventually were successful. But what did we get instead? We got mandatory minimums, truth in sentencing, three strikes. I make this point because one of the really bizarre aspects of the prison system is the way it so easily assimilates "prison reforms" into processes that strengthen it and render it even more repressive than before the reforms were instituted. This is why I always try to disassociate myself and other prison abolitionists from prison reform. Obviously it is important to make life better for people who are in prison. We support reforms that will make life more livable for prisoners, while we call for the abolition of prisons as the default solution for the social problems that prison presumes to solve but cannot.

Many mandatory-minimum sentencing laws emerged precisely as part of the so-called war on drugs, which parallels and bolsters the war on terrorism today. The global war on drugs is responsible for the soaring numbers of people behind bars—and for the fact that throughout the world there is a disproportionate number of people of color and people from the global South in prison. Whom do we discover behind bars in Rome? We find disproportionate numbers of African women, women who have become involved in drug trafficking because it's their only hope. Or because someone promises them $100 to deliver a package. Even in those countries like the Netherlands and the Scandinavian countries where you expect to see only white people, whom do you see? People from Indonesia, the Caribbean, Latin America, and Africa.

The drug war and the war on terror are linked to the global expansion of the prison. This carceral machinery will never be re-formed in more humane ways. Let us remember that the prison is a historical system of punishment. In other words, it has not always been a part of human history; therefore, we should not take this institution for granted, or consider it a permanent and unavoidable fixture of our society. The prison as punishment emerged around the time of industrial capitalism, and it continues to have a particular affinity with capitalism. So continue to engage in grassroots activism against mandatory minimums, and continue to encourage a broader understanding of the political economy of prisons as it is related to larger issues of class exploitation, racism, patriarchy, and heterosexism.

Since the struggles against globalization and for peace are now so important, how can we begin to define those struggles so we can set an agenda?

I don't think there is one single answer to your question. Whatever we are doing, wherever we are, it is imperative that we believe in the possibility of change. We cannot allow ourselves to be ensconced in the present, so the very first step is to actively imagine possible futures—futures beyond the prison and beyond capitalism. So whether you are a student, a trade unionist, or a community activist, you can urge people to incorporate issues related to globalization and peace into their own agendas of action. Globalization has not only created devastating conditions for people in the global South, it has created impoverished and incarcerated communities in the United States and elsewhere in the global North. Labor activists can attempt to generate support for prisoners who are increasingly recruited to do the work of generating profit. They can build campaigns that reveal the ways in which the cheap labor pools in the southern regions are replicated when companies are seduced by prison labor. Despite many historical efforts to organize prison labor unions, prison labor is not organized, and there are no benefits for companies to worry about. All in all, the most important dimension of anti-globalization work for justice and peace involves the expansion of people's awareness of these complicated connections.

With all the conservative backlash, do you think racism is always going to be perpetuated in this country?

An important subtext of my remarks this evening is that we are always more or less complicit in the conditions we contest. For example, I cannot deny that I enjoy criticizing George Bush. I even like to make fun of him. But I must also ask myself whether I did everything in my power to help prevent his election—or non-election. If I acknowledge that I am also implicated in the continued patterns of racism, I ask not only how do I help to change those whom I hold responsible for the structures of racism, I ask also: How do I change myself? The last time I spoke here at Metro State College—in 1993—many people did not want to hear me speak about prisons. "Why do you want to talk about prisons? About criminals? Why are you so concerned about them?" But by shifting the focus to the prison-industrial complex, the discussion could be shifted to another register, which made it possible for people to think about structural racism. Although racism still exercises vast material and ideological influence, we have come a long way in generating the vocabularies for popular engagements with racism. That is something we can applaud. On the other hand, we have not come very far in our defense of affirmative action. In fact, many liberals who opposed the conservative campaign against affirmative action did as much or more damage with respect to the persistence of racism. Some of them said, "We do need to help black people, they do need special attention," without realizing that their defense of affirmative action calls upon the same terms as the conservatives. It's another case of friends doing the work of the enemy.

What about the campaign to free Mumia Abu-Jamal?
Many people responded to 9/11 by decelerating much of their political activism, especially around issues that seemed to be linked to the hornet's nest of issues swirling around the war on terror. Calls for the death of those responsible for the attacks led to a deceleration of anti–capital punishment work. Recognizing this, we can say that it is more important than ever to accelerate the campaign to free Mumia Abu-Jamal and

to accelerate our efforts against the death penalty generally. Over the years, we had been making significant progress in our campaign to abolish the death penalty. One of the most dramatic signs of this progress was the moratorium declared in Illinois. Mumia's case has become the radical face of the movement to abolish the death penalty, not only in the United States but all over the world. Especially since Mumia is often lumped together with terrorists, we have to insist that the media not demonize Mumia. He should not be made into the enemy simply because he was charged with the death of a policeman. The police are not always innocent, and those charged with assault on a policeman are not always guilty.

I am you glad you raised this question, because suddenly, in the aftermath of 9/11, the policeman is the national figure. I say "policeman" in a gender-specific formulation because I am referring to a male figure. I am not trying to demonize policemen and women—there are those who try to do the right thing. But when you consider that the post-9/11 figure of national salvation is the policeman, who in movement circles and communities of color historically stands for racism and repression, the ideological dimension of this national praise of the police becomes clear. Several days ago the U.S. Second Court of Appeals overturned the conviction of three of the four police officers who had been convicted of sodomizing Abner Louima with a broomstick.

How can we follow the lead of the international movement to free Mumia? In France, hundreds of thousands of people have marched in support of Mumia. He was recently declared an honorary citizen of Paris, the first person to be so declared since Pablo Picasso in the early 1970s. In this country we have a major responsibility. This is the only industrialized country in the world that uses the death penalty as a routine for the kinds of offenses for which people in other countries do eight to ten years. This is not to justify acts of harm against human beings. The point is simply that capital punishment is a form of retribution that history has declared obsolete. Moreover, many people are on death row for crimes committed when they were children; others are mentally ill people. Mumia's case is so important not only because he has become a symbol of resistance to the death penalty, but also because he himself has used his skills as a journalist to participate in movements for justice and equality. The most important way to claim this country as our own is to claim it through struggle, to improve it, to use it as an arena where we strive to create a better world.

FIVE

Radical Multiculturalism

Boulder, Colorado
March 1, 2005

I have been asked to craft my remarks this evening in relation to the general rubric of multiculturalism. I thus begin by challenging self-evident meanings of this term, which prevent us from questioning whether we do indeed inhabit a multicultural democracy. Examples of this new multiculturalism are increasingly drawn from the composition of corporate leadership and of government, even, and perhaps especially, from the second administration of George W. Bush, who recently appointed the first black woman, Condoleezza Rice, to serve as Secretary of State of the United States of America. As our observances of Black History Month have just drawn to a close and we inaugurate Women's History Month today, it might be appropriate to venture a few remarks on the sometimes problematic commemoration of "firsts"—the first black person to do this, the first woman to do that. I would gladly relinquish the celebration of the first black woman National Security Adviser, now the first black woman Secretary of State, in exchange for a white male Secretary of State who might provide guidance on how to halt the U.S. global drive for empire, the racist war on terror, and the military aggression against the Iraqi people.

Popular representations of black history, Chicano/a history, women's history over the last decades often have been anchored to the practice of identifying those who become the first of their race or gender associated with particular accomplishments. Conventional notions of multiculturalism rely on a construction of race and gender assimilation that leave existing structures intact. Although Condoleezza Rice was preceded by a black man, Colin Powell, in the position of Secretary of State, their tenure in the office has not made—and is not likely to make—any substantive difference. There are no compelling arguments to be made here about political progress. Yet there are those who invoke Rice and Attorney General Alberto Gonzales as evidence of the perfect multicultural nation: people of color in the very highest positions of government! If I were a participant in such conversations, I would add: people of color who have finally earned the right to contribute to the process of subjugating populations of countries in the global South; people of color who represent the most conservative and most militaristic political positions; people of color who justify torture by referring to the Geneva Convention as "quaint" and "obsolete" in the era of global war against terrorism.

I propose that we bring the terms "democracy" and "freedom" into the frame of our discussion of multiculturalism. As we question and criticize the official meanings of these three principles, we will do so in the hopes of discovering more nuanced, more substantive, more expansive understandings of freedom, democracy, and multiculturalism. You are welcome to construe my remarks as a contribution to the ongoing debate sparked by Professor Ward Churchill's analysis of the global circumstances surrounding the tragedy of September 11, 2001. But my concern is not so much with the event itself, but rather with the way in which this tragedy was opportunistically exploited for the purpose of extending and consolidating the U.S. quest for global dominance.

Why, in the aftermath of September 11, 2001, have we allowed our government to pursue unilateral policies and practices of global war? Why have the official meanings of freedom and democracy and multiculturalism become increasingly restrictive? Why have they become so restrictive that it is difficult to disentangle their official meanings from the meaning of capitalism? If I had the time I would read for you two of George W. Bush's recent speeches—the State of the Union and the Inaugural address—systematically replacing the worlds "freedom" and "democracy" with the word "capitalism." I can guarantee you that this exercise will prove enlightening with respect to current U.S. foreign policy,

Increasingly, freedom and democracy are envisioned by the government as exportable commodities, commodities that can be sold or imposed upon entire populations whose resistances are aggressively suppressed by the military. The so-called global war on terror was devised as a direct response to the September 11 attacks. Donald Rumsfeld, Dick Cheney, and George W. Bush swiftly transformed the attacks on the World Trade Center and the Pentagon into occasions to misuse and manipulate collective grief, thereby reducing this grief to a national desire for vengeance. I am far more distressed by their actions than I am by Ward Churchill's remarks about 9/11. Likewise, I am far more troubled by the Bush government strategies that have led to the deaths of untold numbers of people in Afghanistan and Iraq, than I am by Ward Churchill's comments. Churchill has been accused of subverting the healing process. But it seems to me the most obvious subversion of the healing process occurred when the Bush administration invaded Afghanistan, then Iraq, and now potentially Iran. All in the name of the human beings who died on September 11. Bloodshed and belligerence in the name of freedom and democracy! Violence and vengance against people of color in the Middle East in defense of a multicultural society at home.

Bush had the opportunity to rehearse this strategy of vengeance and death on a smaller scale before he moved into the White House. As governor of Texas, he not only lauded capital punishment, he presided over more executions—152 to be precise—than any other governor in the history of the United States of America. To people who have suffered trauma and lost family members and friends, he offered state-sanctioned killing as a means of coping with their sorrow. Alberto Gonzales was general counsel of Texas for fifty-seven of these death penalty cases, and in each case—including that of a death-row prisoner who was severely mentally disabled—Alberto Gonzales counseled Bush to go forward with the execution.

Imperialist war militates against freedom and democracy, yet freedom and democracy are repeatedly invoked by the purveyors of global war. Precisely those forces that presume to make the world safe for freedom and democracy are now spreading war and torture and capitalist exploitation around the globe. The Bush government represents its project as a global offensive against terrorism, but the conduct of this offensive has generated practices of state violence and state terrorism in comparison to which its targets pale.

Since the period of Black Reconstruction, black Americans and their allies have waged an ongoing battle for the right to vote. In the course of that struggle countless numbers of people have lost their lives to racist terror—including James Chaney, Andrew Goodman, and Michael Schwerner during the 1960s voter registration campaign in the state of Mississippi. This long history of struggle has emphasized the importance of voting rights to the overall workings of democracy. This is why we claim that the last two presidential elections were far from democratic. Not only did the massive disenfranchisement of black men who had previously served time play a decisive role in the outcomes, but beyond felony disenfranchisement, there was also massive voter fraud. In Ohio, for example, polling booths were abundant in affluent communities, but they were so rare in poor black communities that many people gave up and went home after waiting in line for three to four hours. This is an illustration of the structural racism that continues to lurk behind public assertions that we now inhabit a multicultural democracy.

However, as crucial as voting rights may be, we have long recognized that the right to vote by itself does not guarantee democracy. It is not and cannot by itself be the paramount evidence of a democratic order. It matters whether candidates are freely selected or whether money determines who runs and who does not. Elections can be subordinated to the power of money, as we in this country have learned during the recent period. It matters whether the voting process unfolds against the backdrop of other political rights and of economic and social justice. It matters greatly if human rights are violated for the purpose of producing an election. It certainly matters if death and devastation, generated on such a colossal scale, including indiscriminate assaults on an entire culture, helped to stage the U.S.-sponsored elections in Iraq. If democracy in Iraq is to be meaningful at all, it must be disengaged from the state violence deployed by the United States in the putative service of democracy.

Those of you who have recently traveled abroad have probably directly witnessed the precipitous decline of this country's reputation. People in other parts of the world—

especially those who have assumed in the past that the United States is the very paragon of democracy—are entirely baffled with respect to U.S. political practices over the last years. I, for one, have been asked many times how I can explain the election and reelection of George W. Bush (even if he was not duly elected the first time). People in other countries have told me that if events were not so tragic, his presence in the White House would be laughable. People around the world are increasingly challenging the official U.S. government project of defending and exporting freedom and democracy. They ask, for example, whether the interrogations at Abu Ghraib, accompanied as they were by torture, sexual abuse of both women and men, and the general violation of human rights and human dignity of those who were allegedly interrogated, are, in fact, a harbinger of a particularly virulent version of democracy the U.S. government wants to defend and export.

How, then, do we reincorporate multiculturalism into this framework of torture and human rights violations in the presumptive service of democracy? Let's return to the immediate aftermath of the attacks on September 11, and survey our memories of the national reaction: choreographed patriotism that produced millions of flags (many made in China) adorning homes, offices, automobiles, clothing, and everything else imaginable. Everyone, regardless of racial and ethnic background, was invited to participate in the display of this multicultural nationalism. Profitable patriotism even led jewelry stores to advertise flag brooches made of rubies, sapphires, and diamonds. The choreographed marketing of nationalism, war, and state terror in response to 9/11 also led to an almost magical makeover of George W. Bush. If we compare media representations of Bush pre– and post–September 11, we see that he evolved from laughingstock to "elder statesman," from a person described as grammatically challenged to a legitimate president portrayed as patriarchal savior of the free world.

This commodified patriotism not only consolidated the new multicultural United States of America, but in the process forged a collective fear of contesting the Bush administration's foreign policy, as the dangerous pieces of the war on terror were being patched together, as racial profiling led to legal and extra-legal assaults on people of Arab, Muslim, and South Asian descent. The consolidation of a multicultural nationalism made it possible to pass the USA PATRIOT Act with neither public discussion at large, nor even serious congressional discussion. When the use of force resolution was brought before Congress, Barbara Lee, who incidentally is my own representative, was the sole congressperson to speak out against this use-of-force resolution. Even John Lewis, the civil rights legend, confessed that he was afraid to be tagged as soft on terrorism. In other words, the price of inclusion in a multicultural democracy, at a time when the political climate was reminiscent of McCarthyism, was explicit assent to Islamophobia, militarism, and state violence.

The consolidation of the multicultural nation was also enabled by the emergence of old-fashioned patriarchy. I specifically address these remarks to the feminists in the house, male and female and other genders, in the hope that others will follow their lead. In the context of this old-fashioned patriarchy, the heroic male is posited as the essence of the nation, while the female is asked to passively embody the nation: male defender, female embodiment. Both George W. and Laura Bush engaged in the ideological manipulation of women of Afghanistan, whose predicament they invoked as justification for a military invasion. Multicultural armed forces invade the country in order to serve as liberators of women of Afghanistan. Their domestic expression of this defense of patriarchy and hetero-sexism can be detected in the turn to marriage—heterosexual marriage—as the panacea for a whole range of social problems. This representation of marriage as the solution to poverty and juvenile delinquency is accompanied by sustained attacks on same-sex relationships and marriages.

In the aftermath of 9/11, the nation was the only type of community offered to people during that period of collective tragedy. During this period, the new multicultural nation took shape, an imagined nation that hailed not only white citizens, but also black, Latina/o, Asian American, and possibly also Native American citizens. However, the closure of the circle of nationalism enacted important exclusions. If some communities historically targeted by racism were brought into the circle of the nation, others were more pertinaciously expelled. These others were Muslim, or people suspected of practicing Islam, Arabs—or people profiled as Arabs—people from the Middle East, from Central Asia, and from South Asia. As this process unfolded, we witnessed a massive buildup of the military-industrial complex. At a time when the collapse of the Socialist community of nations should have led to further disarmament and to a diminishing role for the Pentagon in the life of this country and of the planet, the Axis of Evil was bellicosely proclaimed, providing justification for many more billions of dollars directed toward the production of weapons.

Multiculturalism by itself does not mark the defeat of racism. That the rise of multiculturalism is proof of the decline of racism is one of those mistaken assumptions that appears to capture the self-evident meaning of multiculturalism. In popular discourse, what this assumption does not acknowledge is the extent to which the terrain of racism has been fundamentally reconfigured. Today, the subterranean, structural dimensions of racism are as influential as ever, even though most people are smart enough to avoid uttering racist statements in public—although this does continue to happen. Moreover, this new terrain of racism is now hugely inflected by ideologies of terrorism. As we have seen, conventional multiculturalism is perfectly compatible with Islamophobia, torture, and violence. A strong multiculturalism, on the other hand, combined with scholarly and popular understandings of racism within the United States and transnationally, addresses the extent to which anti-Muslim and anti-Arab racisms have been incorporated into new structures of repression and punishment. A colossal punishment industry has already claimed the lives of millions of people, overwhelmingly people of color—those who are forced to or have been forced to live inside the country's state prisons, federal prisons, county jails, Indian country jails, immigrant detention centers, as well as the military prisons. In the last few years, racism directed against Muslim and Arab people has been rapidly assimilated into political and legal structures: The PATRIOT Act, initially represented as a legislative appendage to the current war against terror, will lead to permanent changes in the ways citizens and non-citizens alike have access to rights and liberties. Moreover, with the creation of the office of Homeland Security, we have seen an unstoppable proliferation of detention centers for immigrants, which are clearly major ingredients of the prison-industrial complex. Had anyone warned you five years ago that we would be living today under the reign of a Department of Homeland Security, you would have probably accused your interlocuter of projecting ideas from the fascist past of Europe onto the future of the United States.

Let us now turn our attention to the appalling photographic images of the abuse perpetrated against people detained by U.S. military personnel at Abu Ghraib in Iraq. Only one year and a half has passed since the release of the photographs, but some people have already forgotten how shocked and traumatized they were when they first saw the pictures. As images of late-nineteenth- and early-twentieth-century lynchings served as undeniable proof of post-slavery, anti-black racism, these Abu Ghraib photographs are visual reminders of the power of the new racism.

What was the ideological context into which these pictures were released? As we all know, one obvious element of racism consists of the learned capacity to ignore individuality at the expense of the generic. What, then, did people actually see in those photographs, especially when some of [the subjects] were depicted wearing hoods? What questions have shaped the practices through which we consumed those images? Today we inhabit an environment that is bombarded and immersed in photographic, cinematic, televised, and, increasingly, digital images. We inhabit a visual world, but have we learned to read and critically engage with those images? To answer my own question, I say no, because we still tend to assume that the meanings of images are, and should be, self-evident.

The widely disseminated video images of Rodney King being beaten by Los Angeles police officers in 1991 were assumed by many to be self-evident proof of police brutality. However, when the police officers involved in the beating, whose mediated images millions had witnessed, went to trial, they were found not guilty. Their defense attorney persuaded the jury that what they were looking at was not a videotape of police beating a black man, but an aggressive, violent black man attacking the police officers, who, in turn were acting in self-defense. Even George H. W. Bush expressed astonishment at the verdict. I mention this case that eventually sparked the 1992 Los Angeles riots in order to urge you to think about the interpretive frameworks that inform our consumption of images. Interpretive frameworks are capable of producing meanings that can appear to be the diametrical opposite of what the images seem to document.

So, if we return to our original questions about the Abu Ghraib photographs, we can add some additional ones: What were the dominant interpretations of these photographs? Did we accept the interpretive framework for the photographs, which was created by the question: does the behavior depicted in the images constitute torture or does it not? Was this the work of a few aberrant individuals, or was it the consequence of decisions made higher up in the chain of command? The overarching question that swirled around the release of these photographs had to do with the nature of American democracy. How did these pictures serve as a comment on the current status of democracy in the United States?

I'm not suggesting that such questions are not important; indeed they are. But other important questions were foreclosed by the collective anxiety regarding U.S. democracy that caused the images of torture and sexual abuse to be positioned within an interpretive framework governed by the need to rescue the idea of democracy. In other words, the discourse around the images had little to do with the individuals who were the subject of the violence depicted. The human content of the images was eradicated precisely in the process of attempting to grapple with the dehumanization represented in the photographs. As consumers of the images, we were not encouraged to focus our attention on the human beings, on the women and men who were subjected to military tortures and sexual coercion. We were encouraged to see them as a mass of naked bodies, piled up in a pyramid; as a hooded figure standing on a box; as anonymous Iraqis forced by female U.S. soldiers to simulate sex with one another. The public interpretation of these images foreclosed the possibility of solidarity with the people whom the soldiers had so profoundly abused.

We were urged to feel so troubled about the implications of these images for U.S. democracy—how to explain, rethink, and rebuild democracy in light of these pictures—that we were not offered an opportunity to experience kinship when the victims' military torture. I have already discussed the foreclosure of global solidarities by the nationalist construction of community in the aftermath of 9/11. At a time when people all over the planet were in solidarity with us, we were encouraged to seek refuge inside the nation, to minimize, not maximize, our outreach. The United States of America has assumed its own supremacy for so long that this assumption of superiority affects the way we think about even our own progressive projects. One of the most damaging aspects of American exceptionalism is that it closes us down and prevents us from imagining ourselves as citizens of the planet. At the beginning of the twenty-first century, we are in dire need of other kinds of globalities, globalities that do not depend on the circuits of capital, globalities that are disentangled from the agendas of global capitalism.

When I saw the Abu Ghraib pictures for the first time, they immediately reminded me of the old photographs of lynchings. I thought about lynching images and the impulse to reproduce and disseminate these ultimate expressions of racist violence. As the soldiers felt impelled to document the horrors they witnessed and choreographed, so did the purveyors of lynchings create visual souvenirs of racist killings that were often transformed into celebratory occasions. The smiling faces of the U.S. soldiers in Abu Ghraib recapitulate the perverse celebrations of lynchings, which became important recreational pastimes in the U.S. South. The photographic images of torture in Iraq recall the postcards of lynching and other visual souvenirs at the beginning of the last century.

Lynching not only extinguished black peoples' lives, it removed them from the possibility of belonging, both to U.S. society and to the human community. The images of both the black lynching victim and the Iraqi prisoner at Abu Ghraib became visual materializations of an ideologically constructed enemy. In both contexts, corporeal and sexual violence played a prominent role. In the U.S. historical context, we discover castrations of lynching victims, the marketing of limbs and members, the carving of fetuses from lynched pregnant women, the racist use of the rape charge to justify lynchings of vast numbers of black men and women. In the photographs of Abu Ghraib, we find coerced simulated sex acts and a pornographic manipulation of the meanings of sexuality in Muslim culture.

In the historical U.S. South and in the U.S.-occupied Iraqi prison, Abu Ghraib, violence is sexualized and sex is rendered unspeakably violent. In both instances, racism enables the coupling of violence and sexuality. Racism is not static. It changes. It mutates. It gets altered by historical circumstances. When we think about new strains of racism, some of them are not so easily identified because we rely on commonsense notions of what counts as racism. Today, we tend to assume that racism involves explicit discrimination, especially as condoned by the law. The historical campaigns associated with the Civil Rights movement led to the eradication of most explicit references to race in the law. It also shifted public expectations such that the expression of racist ideas are no longer condoned within the public sphere. If we are unable to identify new contemporary modes of racism, we render those who are its targets even more vulnerable that they may have been previously.

The U.S. public seemed to treat the perverse abuse and coercion in the Iraqi prison as so aberrant, so egregious that no analogous set of circumstances could be found in the nation's history. Comparisons with lynching were never raised or acknowledged in most popular discussions of the crimes documented in the Abu Ghraib photos. Histories of racism in the United States reveal numerous conjunctures of race, sex, and violence. Consider the sexual abuse inside U.S. prisons, whose populations are more "multicultural" than student and faculty populations at most colleges and universities. I am not referring to spectacular examples of sexual violence, but rather the undramatic and routine sexual assaults that are woven into quotidian prison regimes. The strip search, the cavity search, and the vaginal and rectal searches to which women are subjected daily by virtue of their incarceration are all forms of institutionalized sexual coercion. Many women who are the targets of these invasive corporeal assaults have said that they experience these invasions of their bodies as no different from an actual rape or sexual assault in less public conditions. They say that it feels like sexual abuse, and if it were not for the uniforms of those who conduct such searches, these activities would be described as sexual abuse. These everyday sexual tortures set the stage for spectacular sexual tortures. We tend to take the former for granted, while the latter shock our conscience.

White women soldiers were implicated in the Baghdad tortures, and many people experienced this as unexpected and shocking. After all, women are not supposed to engage in torture or sexual coercion. On the other hand, within the formalistic framework associated with capitalist democracy, women achieve equality by having equal access to all areas dominated by men; including equal access to the military, perhaps even equal access to engage in torture and coercion. Such formalism recalls the logic of conventional multiculturalism. If we simply demand equal access for people of color to the military, equal access of women to combat, equal access of gays and lesbians to the military, we end up supporting a superficial multiculturalism that allows the institutions it supposedly transforms to continue to function in the old way, except that the purveyors of dehumanization are not only white men. Instead of transforming dominant culture, dominant culture enlists new sectors to impose itself and perpetuate its ways.

Even in the descriptions of tortures inflicted on Iraqi prisoners, there are noxious strains of racism, some of which are not so easily recognizable because they rely on generally accepted commonsense ideas. These include the trivialization of Islamic cultural leaders and the wielding of cultural misunderstandings as political weapons. The promulgation of Samuel P. Huntington's notion of a clash of civilizations relies on racist justifications for wars for global dominance masquerading as a war on terror. Civilizational thinking creates cultural hierarchies and the inevitable quest for superiority.

The global reputation of U.S. democracy has declined precisely in proportion to the extent to which the language of democracy is deployed as a rhetorical weapon in the quest for empire. What is most distressing to those of us who believe in a democratic future is the tendency to equate democracy with capitalism. Capitalist democracy should be recognized as the oxymoron that it is. The two orders are fundamentally incompatible, especially considering the contemporary transformations of capitalism under the impact of globalization. But there are those who cannot tell the difference between the two. The model of democracy associated with capitalism is free enterprise, although free enterprise does not capture the state of capitalism today. Moreover, in no historical era can the freedom of the market serve as an acceptable model of democracy for those who do not possess the means—the capital—to take advantage of the freedom of the market. Karl Marx revealed the manipulations underlying the equation of capitalism and democracy in chapter 6 of Volume I of *Capital*.

The most convincing contemporary evidence against the equation of capitalism and democracy can be discovered in the fact that many institutions with a profoundly democratic impulse have been dismantled under the pressure exerted by international financial agencies, such as the International Monetary Fund and the World Bank. In the global South, structural adjustment has unleashed a juggernaut of privatization of public services that used to be available to masses of people, such as education and health care. These are services that no society should deny its members, services we all should be able to claim by virtue of our humanity. Yet our system of capitalism eschews economic democracy even as it proclaims itself to be the vanguard of democracy around the world. Conservative demands to privatize Social Security in the United States further reveal the reign of profits for the few over the rights of the many.

I want to conclude by evoking in broad outlines the social justice movements that are developing around the world. The opposition to U.S. militarism in the context of anti-globalization campaigns is accompanied by an awareness of the interrelatedness of war and profit. These movements are offering us important alternatives to superficial notions of multiculturalism. At the recent World Social Forum in Porto Alegre, Brazil, organizers, labor activists, students, cultural workers and concerned people proclaimed that they are not afraid to dream about the possibility of a better world. They do not engage race and gender in isolation from issues of economic democracy and social justice. They say that a non-exploitative, non-racist, democratic economic order is possible. They say that new social relations are possible, ones that link human beings around the planet not by the commodities some produce and others consume, but rather by equality and solidarity and cooperation and respect. This, in my opinion, would help to define a radical multiculturalism, as opposed to a superficial multiculturalism that simply calls for diversity in the service of exploitation and war. Another world is possible, and despite the hegemony of forces that promote inequality, hierarchy, possessive individualism, and contempt for humanity, I believe that together we can work to create the conditions for radical social transformation.

SIX

Abolition Democracy

December 2, 2005
Oakland, California

Serendipitously, this meeting takes place on December 2, International Day for the Abolition of Slavery as designated by the United Nations. Throughout the world people are observing this day by reflecting on the continued presence of slavery on our planet—especially in the form of the trafficking of human beings—and by rededicating themselves to the project of abolishing slavery. In a message released today, UN Secretary General Kofi Annan said: "People who perpetrate, condone, or facilitate slavery or slavery-like practices must be held accountable by national and, if necessary, international means." "The international community," he said, "must also do more to combat poverty, social exclusion, illiteracy, ignorance, and discrimination, which increase vulnerability and are part of the underlying context for this scourge."

As this benefit for the Pacific radio station KPFA is a book launch for *Abolition Democracy: Beyond Empire, Prisons and Torture* (and I will be reading passages from the book), I want to consider how to articulate a triple abolition: abolition of the death penalty; abolition of the prison-industrial complex, including its military components with their technologies of torture and terror; and abolition of the sediments of slavery that have been sustained by capital punishment and the prison system. Issues raised by abolition, especially when we consider the abolition of slavery as organically linked to the abolition of prisons and capital punishment, help us to recognize the pitfalls of abstract equality and formal democracy. One of the glaring contradictions enabled by the cohabitation of poverty and racism, on the one hand, and legal equality and democracy, on the other, can be found in the soaring population behind bars and the cavalier manner in which increasing numbers of people are being put to death.

This morning at 2:00 a.m. Eastern Time, when Kenneth Lee Boyd was executed by the state of North Carolina, he became the one-thousandth person to be put to death since the reinstatement of the death penalty in 1976. Just a few hours ago, Shawn Humphries was executed in South Carolina. Wesley Baker is scheduled to be executed in the next few days in Maryland. And then there is the death chamber at San Quentin Prison, which is scheduled to be used on December 13 to extinguish the life of Stanley Tookie Williams. For the last twenty-five years of his life, Stanley has been in prison refashioning himself and reaching out to others. An autodidact, he has published nine books, including eight that are specifically addressed to children and designed to direct them toward productive futures rather than gang life. He has also given lectures by telephone to schoolchildren and youth of all ages. As a result of his Protocol for Street Peace, which has been used by rival gangs around the country and the world, he has been nominated for the Nobel Peace Prize. Moreover, he also received the President's Call to Service Award. Let us redouble our efforts here in the Bay Area to prevent our state from killing him.

Over the last decade, capital punishment has become more

and more rationalized and routinized. Thirty-five years ago, in 1970, I myself faced the death penalty, having been charged with three capital crimes: murder, kidnapping, and conspiracy. During that period, the death penalty was applied in what was clearly intended to be an openly racist fashion. In 1972, capital punishment was temporarily abolished in California, and in 1973, the U.S. Supreme Court ruled in the *Furman v. Georgia* case that the application of the death penalty was unconstitutional. Death penalty abolitionists greeted this decision as a major triumph, but, as it turned out, it was a pyrrhic victory. Three years later the Supreme Court's ruling in *Gregg v. Georgia* declared that death sentences were constitutional if they were meted out in accordance with what the Supreme Court called guided discretion.

Current guidelines for the application of the death penalty are now quite rational. They reflect the abstract individualism associated with liberalism and especially neoliberalism. They reflect the rather simplistic assumption that the death penalty ceases to be a punishment informed by racism when it is equally extended to white people. Equality prevails when executions become equal opportunity punishments. Five years into the twenty-first century, there are indeed more white people on death row. As a matter of fact, the executions I mentioned earlier, with the exception of the planned execution of Tookie Williams, were all state killings of white men.

This notion that formal equality is a harbinger of a better world is deeply flawed, which means that under no circumstances can the sentencing of a white person to death—even, as in the case of James Byrd, for killing a black person—be considered a sign of progress. But let me turn to another example of the pitfalls of abstract equality. In the conversations with Eduardo Mendieta in *Abolition Democracy*, he asked me about the photographs of torture and sexual coercion at Abu Ghraib and what he called "the equal-opportunity, racial-sexual torture contract" in which gender equality is construed as equal opportunity to wield the weapons of violence controlled by the state. What was most shocking to many people who viewed the photographs was the fact that women soldiers were as involved in the sexual violence as their male counterparts. This was supposed to be impossible; women were not supposed to be capable of inflicting sexual violence on prisoners. This was my response:

"The representations of women soldiers were quite dramatic, and most people found them utterly shocking. But we might also say that they provided powerful evidence of what the most interesting feminist analyses have tried to explain: that there is a difference between the body gendered as female and the set of discourses and ideologies that inform the sex/gender system. These images were a kind of visualization of this sex/gender conjunction. We are not accustomed to visually apprehending the difference between female bodies and male supremacist ideologies. Therefore seeing images of a woman engaged in behavior that we associate with male dominance is startling. But it should not be, especially if we take seriously what we know about the social construction of gender. Especially within institutions that rely on ideologies of male dominance, women can be easily mobilized to commit the same acts of violence expected of men—just as black people, by virtue of being black, are not therefore immune from the charge of promoting racism."

I went on to say: "The images to which you're referring evoke a memory of a comment made by Colin Powell during the first Gulf War. He said that the military was the most democratic institution in our society and created a framework in which people could escape the constraints of race and, we can add today, gender as well. This notion of the military as a leveling institution, one that constitutes each member as equal, is frightening and dangerous, because you must eventually arrive at the conclusion that this equality is about equal opportunity to kill, to torture, to engage in sexual coercion.

"At the time I found it very bizarre that Powell would point to the most hierarchal institution, with its rigid chain of command, as the epitome of democracy. Today, I would say that such a conception of democracy reveals the problems and limitations of civil rights strategies and discourses.

"This is true not only with respect to race and gender, but with respect to sexuality as well. Why is the effort to challenge sexism and homophobia in the military largely defined by the question of admission to existing hierarchies and not also a powerful critique of the institution itself? Equality might be considered to be the equal right to refuse and resist.

"How might we consider the visual representation of female bodies collaborating in acts of sexual torture—forcing Arab men to engage in public masturbation, for example—as calling for a feminist analysis that challenges prevailing assumptions that the only possible relationship between women and violence requires women to be the victims?

"When one looks at certain practices often unquestionably accepted by women guards in U.S. prisons, one can glimpse the potential for the sexual coercion that was at the core of the torture strategies at Abu Ghraib. I return, therefore, to the question of those established circuits of violence in which both women and men participate, the techniques of racism administered not only by white people, but by black, Latino, Native American, and Asian people as well. Today we might say that we have all been offered an equal opportunity to perpetuate male dominance and racism.

"I return, therefore, to the question of those established circuits of violence in which both women and men participate, the techniques of racism administered not only by white people, but by black, Latino, Native American, and Asian people as well. Today we might say that we have all been offered an equal opportunity to perpetuate male dominance and racism."

Thus, people in power, regardless of gender or race, have an equal opportunity to inflict racist and sexist violence on others. This may be the most important message implied in our "diverse" government. I enclose the term in quotes because the very term "diversity" prevents people from thinking seriously and deeply about the extent to which our institutions are thoroughly saturated with racism, sexism, homophobia, class bias, and xenophobia. According to George Bush, who likes to congratulate himself for being the president of a diverse country, diversity is a very good thing, especially as long as it does not rock the boat. During his first visit to Brazil, he indicated that he had not previously been aware that there was such a large population of black people there. Not long ago he made a second visit and was sufficiently well-informed when he spoke with the president, Lula da Silva to characterize both Brazil and the United States as "diverse" societies. It seems that he likes using that word.

When Eduardo and I began to talk about the problem of the Bush presidency, Eduardo said, "I think there is a kind of identification between the American public and the president. It is just staggering that despite Bush's lying, deception, and manipulation, he manages to get reelected. When officers and presidents can trample on truth and law, we are in the midst of empire." This is what I said:

"A moral panic was generated by 9/11 and the subsequent specter of terrorism, which puts security at the center of all conversations, both conversations in favor of the war on Iraq and conversations in opposition to the war on Iraq. This focus on security as internal and external policing helps to manufacture the ubiquitous fear that causes people to ignore those dimensions of security that would require attention to such issues as health care, education, and housing, for example.

"The problem of the presidency is not primarily a question of deceit—most people, regardless of their political affiliations, and regardless of their level of education, take for granted the fact that politicians lie and deceive. That is the nature of the game, and I am not sure that Bush is distinguished by his capacity to deceive. Bush was reelected precisely because of the panic generated by the September 11 attacks and because of the ease with which we were all entranced by the images and rhetoric of nationalism associated with claims of U.S. citizenship. American exceptionalism is taken for granted and there is no popular discourse that allows us to understand that the superiority of the United States is grounded in exploitation and repression.

"Why were we so quick to imagine the nation as the limit of human solidarity, precisely at a moment when people all over the world identified with our pain and suffering? Why was it not possible to receive that solidarity in a way that allowed us to return it and to imagine ourselves more broadly as citizens of the world? This would have allowed for the inclusion of people within the United States not legally defined as 'citizens.'

"The production of the nation as the primary mode of solidarity was exclusionary, excluding those within and without who were not legally citizens. The brutal attacks on people who appeared to be Muslim or Arab announced that racism was very much alive in the United States and striking out at new targets. So I suppose I am more concerned about the ease with which this moral panic emerged than I am about presidential dishonesty and deception."

And if you remember four years ago, how quickly so many people who considered themselves to be progressive and radical took refuge in this idea that we as Americans had to consolidate ourselves as a militarized nation, which inevitably meant excluding all of those who were not Americans.

As a matter of fact, many people of color felt very proud that they were now included under the mantle of Americanism. An acquaintance of mine who has a dual passport—actually, she has citizenship in the United States, in Ghana, and in Britain—said she came back shortly after September 11, and for the very first time in her life, when the immigration officials saw her passport, they said to her, "Welcome home."

I return to the conversation with Eduardo: "During the period before the international collapse of socialism, there existed the practice of designating those communities fighting for the rights of labor, against racism, for justice, peace, and equality, as the "Other America." Today, it seems that many of us who oppose the policies and practices of the Bush administration are still, at bottom, greatly influenced by the ideology of American exceptionalism. Thus the sense of paralysis in the aftermath of September 11, and the dangerous embrace of the worst kind of nationalism."

"This disturbs me," I said to him, "more than anything else, because if we are to have hope for a better future, we will have to be capable of imagining ourselves citizens of a new global order, which may very well include our acceptance of leadership from people in Iraq and others engaged in frontline battles. This may appear to be nostalgia," I said to him, "for a political past that was less complicated than our present times, but actually," I said, "I am attempting to acknowledge the ways in which we sometimes tend to rely on the ideologies we think we are opposing. One of our main challenges is to reconceptualize the notion of security. How can we make the world secure from the ravages of global capitalism? This broad sense of security might involve debt relief for Africa. It would mean an end to the juggernaut of privatization that threatens a new society, that, for example, people in South Africa have been trying to build. It would involve the shifting of priorities from the prison-industrial complex to education, housing, health care. Bush was elected the second time precisely because of the moral panic that diverted people's attention away from the more complicated questions about our future. Bush was elected not only because of the fear of another terrorist attack but because of the fear that American global superiority may be on the wane."

When Eduardo asked me a question about the relationship between the production of law and the violation of law in the United States, I answered in this way: "The convoluted legalistic vocabulary produced by the war on terror would make great material for comedy if it did not have such brutal consequences. These new categories have been deployed as if they have a long history in law and common usage—as if they are self-evident—and their strategic effects of circumventing the Geneva Conventions and a host of human rights instruments have once again relied on the notion that the United States stands above the UN, the World Court, and everything else."

And then I went on to say, "I wonder whether this subterfuge doesn't point to a more general problem, that of the new political discourse generated by the Bush administration. The Bush vocabulary, which pretends to express complicated ideas in the simplest and most unsophisticated terms, is both seductive and frightening. It is seductive because it appears to require no effort to understand; it is dangerous because it erases everything that really matters. Just as the meaning of enemy combatant is assumed to be self-evident, so are the meanings of the terms 'freedom' and 'democracy.'

"This leveling of political discourse to the extent that it is not supposed to require any effort to understand—that it appears self-evident, incontrovertible, and logical—enables aggression and injury. This is true of the simplistic, often crude vocabulary that Bush tends to use, it is true of his repetition of the words freedom and democracy in ways that empty them of serious content, and it is true of his representation of terrorists as 'evildoers.' But it is also true of such legalistic notions as 'enemy combatant' and 'extraordinary rendition.' "

Because extraordinary rendition describes a process of transporting prisoners to other countries for the purpose of having them interrogated. What the term hides is that the countries to which these prisoners are rendered are known to employ torture. And, of course, we recently learned about the secret CIA prisons in Eastern Europe.

Later in our conversation, we spoke about W. E. B. DuBois and abolition democracy. DuBois argued that the abolition of slavery was accomplished only in the negative sense. "In order to achieve the *comprehensive* abolition of slavery—after the institution was rendered illegal and black people were released from their chains—new institutions should have been created to incorporate black people into the social order. The idea that every former slave was supposed to receive forty acres and a mule is sometimes mocked as an unsophisticated rumor that circulated among slaves. Actually, this notion originated in a military order that conferred abandoned Confederate lands to freed black people in some parts of the South. But the continued demand for land and the animals needed to work it reflected an understanding among former slaves that slavery could not be truly abolished until people were provided with the economic means for their subsistence. They also needed access to educational institutions and needed to claim voting and other political rights, a process that had begun, but remained incomplete, during the short period of radical reconstruction that ended in 1877."

DuBois argues that a host of democratic institutions are needed to fully achieve abolition—thus abolition democracy. "If we think about capital punishment as an inheritance of slavery, its abolition would also involve the creation of those institutions about which DuBois wrote, institutions that still remain to be built 140 years after the end of slavery. If we link the abolition of capital punishment to the abolition of prisons, then we have to be willing to let go of the alternative of life without possibility of parole as the primary alternative. And thinking specifically about the problem of prisons, using the approach of abolition democracy, we would propose the creation of an array of social institutions that would begin to solve the social problems that set people on the track to prison, thereby helping to render the prison obsolete."

Many people do not want to oppose the death penalty unless they can be guaranteed that those who therefore escape capital punishment will be kept in prison for the rest of their lives. That is to say, instead of suffering corporeal death, that of the body, they will suffer the civil death of imprisonment. "There is," I said to him, "a direct connection with slavery. When slavery was abolished, black people were set free, but they lacked access to the material resources that would enable them to fashion new and free lives. Prisons have thrived over the last century precisely because of the absence of those resources and the persistence of some of the deep structures of slavery. They cannot, therefore, be eliminated until new institutions and resources are made available to those communities that provide in part the human beings that make up the prison population."

Capital punishment should have been abolished and might well have been abolished had not slavery continued to be a major force in this country. During the period of the American Revolution, there was a great deal of debate about capital punishment, which could be the penalty for a wide range of crimes including arson, counterfeiting, rape, robbery, and even horse theft. Benjamin Franklin, Benjamin Rush and others considered it archaic and barbaric, arguing that it had no place in a democratic society. Most states did eventually abolish capital punishment for most crimes lesser than murder (and in some cases rape). However, within slave law, the death sentence continued to be inflicted on enslaved people for very minor offenses. Thus, in effect, the death penalty was abolished for minor offenses only for white people. It was a thoroughly racialized abolition. Abolitionists continually pointed out that in Virginia, for example, a white man could be punished by death only if he had committed murder, but a slave could be subject to the death penalty for more than seventy different offenses. Slavery became a refuge for the death penalty, where it was also preserved as an ordinary and routine mode of punishment.

In the aftermath of slavery, the death penalty that was an integral part of slave law was gradually deracialized; it entered the law at large in such a way that its seemingly obvious connection with slavery was subject to erasure. Today, the death penalty has been evacuated of the historical racism that produced it. It is true that there is a hugely disproportionate number of black people and people of color on death rows all over the country, and it is also true that a person has a greater likelihood of being sentenced to death if his or her victims are white. While it is important to acknowledge and contest these racist modes through which the death penalty is applied, it is perhaps even more important to understand the structural racism there that emerged from its connection with slavery.

Let's back up and say a few words about racism in the contemporary era, that is, racism in what is often referred to as the post–civil rights era, especially since Rosa Parks has been inducted into the pantheon of our national heroes. While I have always deeply respected Rosa Parks, I was extremely ambivalent about the Bush government decision to have her body placed for viewing in the Capitol Rotunda, the first woman to receive this honor. Proclaiming her to be a national hero was tantamount to declaring the struggle against racism to have ended in ultimate triumph. Rosa Parks's body has been transmuted into a symbol of victory over racial injustice and inequality. Alive, she would have certainly insisted that the struggle continues. *A luta continua.*

There are persisting structures of racism, economic and political structures that do not openly display their discriminatory strategies, but nonetheless serve to keep communities of color in a state of inferiority and oppression.

"Therefore," I said in my conversations with Eduardo, "I think about the death penalty as incorporating the historical inheritances of racism within the framework of a legal system that has been evacuated of overt racism while continuing to provide a haven for the inheritances of racism. This is how it can be explained that capital punishment is still very much alive in a country that presents itself as the paragon for democracy in the world. There are more than 3,500 U.S. citizens currently on death row in the United States, at a time"—and I should say that not all 3,500 are legally U.S. citizens. "There are more than 3,500 people on death row in the United States at a time when all European countries have abolished capital punishment, when the European Union makes the abolition of the death penalty a precondition for membership."

Turkey has recently abolished its death penalty in order to enter into the European Union. Côte d'Ivoire just abolished its death penalty. Senegal just abolished its death penalty. As a matter of fact, it is now the trend in Africa to abolish capital punishment, following South Africa. Capital punishment is a receptacle for the legacies of racism. But now, under the rule of legal equality, it can apply its lethal power to anyone, regardless of their racial background.

It is interesting how much more difficult it is to transform discourses than it is to build new institutions. Many decades after the fiction of black unity was exposed, the most popular assumption within black communities continues to be that unity alone will bring progress. Even now, when we can point to people like Condoleezza Rice and Clarence Thomas, people retain this dream of unity. Young people who are just beginning to develop a sense of themselves in the world assume that the only way they can make a better future for the many black people who lead economically and intellectually impoverished lives is by uniting the entire black community. I hear this repeatedly.

What would be the purpose of uniting the entire black community? How would one possibly bring people together across all the complicated lines of politics and class? It would be futile to try to create a single black community today. But it does make sense, I said, "to think about organizing communities, organizing communities not simply around their blackness, but primarily around political goals. Political struggle has never been so much a question about how it is identified or chooses to identify as it has been a question of how one thinks race, gender, class, sexuality affect the way human relations are constructed in the world."

SEVEN

Racism: Then and Now

University of Washington, Seattle
April 17, 2007

Before I begin this evening, I would like to acknowledge the tragic events that happened at Virginia Tech University yesterday morning. I'd like to say that I know that all of us deeply empathize with the families and friends of the people who were killed on that campus. This was the worst mass shooting, apparently, in the history of this country. But as we symbolically express our sympathies to the families and friends of the dead students, we should reflect on the extent to which violence has become a normal mode of behavior in this country, made easily available as a mode of expression for a range of psychological or emotional disorders. I'm beginning this way because I'm very concerned about the interpretive context that has been created for us.

I checked my email just before coming this evening and discovered a message from a higher-up where I teach regarding security measures on the campus. I'm concerned that we're now being asked to accept as a solution to that horrible tragedy increased security measures. I'd like us to reflect on what it means to witness the growing development of something we might call the security state, a security state that relies on our collective fear. We fear terrorists, and therefore we assent to a global war on terror. We feared communists; I should say that *they* feared communists because I was one of the communists they feared. We also fear crime, and therefore there are ever more prisons, ever larger numbers of people incarcerated, ever larger numbers of people put to death.

This horrible tragedy in Virginia has made me wonder what it is that instructs our fear. Why is it that we learn to fear terrorism but not racism, not sexism, not homophobia? I wonder why we don't fear a president who is at the helm of a twenty-first-century drive for global American empire. I wonder why we don't fear the distorted way in which democracy is being defined under the auspices of the current administration. And I wonder why we don't fear privatization. We could talk about all of the social services that have been privatized. We could talk about the privatization of war as well. We could talk about what Naomi Klein has called "disaster capitalism." In the immediate aftermath of Katrina, I was joking with some friends and I said, "The next thing you know, Halliburton is going to be in New Orleans." I was laughing about it. And then, of course, there they were.

I think it might be important for us to reflect on what it is that shapes and elicits and defines our fear. This evening I've been asked to talk about civil rights, human rights, the unfinished work of the struggle for equality here in the United States, and the connections with other struggles, the transnational dimensions.

I'll begin by saying that we are, at the beginning of the twenty-first century, continuing to live the history that we often relegate to the past. At a time when many of the political leaders in this country, and the majority of the Supreme Court justices, argue that precisely because racial justice has been achieved, affirmative action is no longer necessary to achieve racial or gender equality, it might be important to think about the meaning of justice, the meaning of racial justice, the meaning of gender justice, and to talk more deeply about race. The principle of color blindness has so saturated our ideas about race that we now tend to believe—at least those who voted to eliminate affirmative action in California, here in Washington, and just recently in Michigan—that the only way to achieve racial justice is to become blind to the work that race does, which means that racism itself gets ignored.

I would like us to think deeply this evening about the extent to which we live with, are influenced by, and in large measure accept racism as a fact of social life. And I would like us to think about what questions we might ask about the various ways racism transforms and becomes something quite different from the racism against which the civil rights movement struggled. That leads me to ask, where does race live? Where does racism live? Where did it reside in the past? And how do we shrink the spaces haunted by racism in order to begin to send it on its way? So we want to talk about something like the migrations of racism. We might ask, to what extent has the so-called war on terror and the current war in Iraq transformed the way racism manifests itself? And why do we have trouble perceiving that racism? Why do we have trouble perceiving the war in Iraq as a racist war?

As I was watching the news about the events at Virginia Tech yesterday, there was a brief report on what happened yesterday in Iraq. Apparently, there were five solders killed yesterday. We learn every day what the death toll is, right? Of course, numbers can't begin to capture the fact that anytime anyone loses his or her life, it's a major tragedy, whether it's five or one hundred people who are harmed. But I'm interested in the fact that we rarely hear the numbers for Iraqi people. Why is that?

As difficult as it might be to move beyond the barrier of those numbers, at least we would have something to work with. And, of course, estimates range from 500,000 to 700,000 so far, and some people say that one million people have been killed during the war in Iraq. Why can't we even have a national conversation about that?

That has a lot to do with the way in which our emotions have been trained and taught by racism. I'm not talking about racism as something that cannot affect those whose bodies are racialized as the target of racist discrimination. You see what I'm saying? All of us sustain these ideological influences. We learn to think in racist terms. How many black women in this lecture hall have ever walked to the other side of the street if they see a young black man with baggy pants, the stereotype?

Racism plays a major role in determining who is subject to state punishment and who is not. How many people are in prison now? Over two million! We always think of numbers as the hard evidence, right? If you have the figures, you know exactly what's going on. But we often fail to think about the mystifying power of numbers. There are approximately 2.2 million people currently incarcerated in county jails, state prisons, federal prisons, Indian country jails, military prisons, and immigrant detention centers. (We do not know how many people the United States incarcerates abroad in its network of secret military prisons.) This means that over the course of a year, there are more than 13 million people who are incarcerated by authorities. When we consider the disproportionate number of people of color among those who are arrested and imprisoned, and the ideological role that imprisonment plays in our lives, I want to suggest that the prison population in this country provides visible evidence of who is not allowed to participate in this democracy, that is to say, who does not have the same rights, who does not enjoy the same liberties, who cannot reach the same level of education and access, who cannot be a part of the body politic, and who is therefore subject to a form of civil death.

The governor of Florida has decided that he's going to push for a change in the laws regarding felony disenfranchisement. Have you heard about that? Why didn't someone do that before the 2000 election? Because it is clear that of the 950,000 people who are disenfranchised in Florida, had a small fraction of them voted, there would have been no question about the defeat of the country's current president. There is a question about the victory, right? I won't say that he was elected, because he wasn't elected. But there would have been no question about the defeat. Of all the states in the U.S., Florida has the largest population of former felons who are disenfranchised: 950,000 people.

People in prison cannot vote. I think it's really strange that we don't question the fact that because you are incarcerated, you should not have the right to vote, you should not be a participant in the political arena, you should be banned, barred. I wonder why that is, because there are quite a few countries where people vote when they're in prison. They just put polls up and let people vote. It used to be that students couldn't vote, and they didn't have polls on campuses. If you didn't go home, where you were registered, there was no way you could vote. Do you remember that? There are actually similarities between universities and prisons. We could pursue them if we wanted to.

But the point that I'm trying to make right now is that prisons tell us that we are free. We are able to recognize ourselves as participants in a democracy because we get to look at this institution that has walled off those who are not. And because there are those who are not, by comparing ourselves to them, we know that we are. In a sense, you might say we know that we are alive, at least politically or civilly alive, by looking at those who have been relegated to civil death.

We inhabit an image environment that is saturated with representations of the prison. It would be interesting to keep a count of how many television programs, movies, and magazine articles you encounter with representations of jail, prison, and detained people. And the saturation of our visual environment leads us to think that we actually have some real knowledge about the issue. But, as a matter of fact, real knowledge about this institution has been marginalized from public consciousness. The media do not educate us about the real, long-term costs and consequences that imprisonment imposes upon us as a nation, as communities, as families, and as citizens and individuals with non-resident status. It does not educate us on how the institution of enslavement has lived on, generation after generation, by influencing how other institutions are administered.

I'm also concerned about the Thirteenth Amendment to the U.S. Constitution and its ability to abolish slavery. We almost treat law as a religion. In fact, there are real connections. Many U.S. courtrooms have four words on the wall: "IN GOD WE TRUST." We believe what the law says; but how can the law abolish an institution that had played such a role in shaping the destiny of this country in so many ways? The Thirteenth Amendment states, "Neither slavery nor involuntary servitude, except as a punishment for crimes whereof the party shall have been duly convicted." That makes it seem that the authors were largely talking about involuntary servitude. Earlier today I was having a conversation with a group of students, and we were questioning the role that the Thirteenth Amendment plays in the history of civil rights in this country.

What did the authors of the Thirteenth Amendment mean

and intend? Were they talking about slavery as human property? Is that what they were talking about? Were they talking about forms of punishment, corporal punishment, all of those forms of punishment associated with slavery? Were they talking about the fact that slavery is non-citizenship? What were they talking about? What is it that they sought to abolish? My people continued to have what we all refer to as second-class citizenship for a long time, right? So I don't think that was what was meant. Or, if the meaning was there, it actually didn't happen. If slavery had been abolished in its entirety, why did it take another hundred years for black people in the South to achieve the right to vote? I can tell you that when I first registered to vote—actually I *tried* to register to vote, because I'm from the South—I wasn't allowed to because I was not literate enough. I didn't pass the test given in Birmingham, Alabama. I suppose I'm arguing that we still live with the vestiges of slavery, which is one explanation for the failure to accord equal rights to all people who live in this country.

What does it mean to have equal rights? As I said before, we implicitly compare those rights with those who do not have rights. So the prisoner becomes the negative measure of what it means to be a participant in civil society, what it means to enjoy civil rights.

Since I was asked to talk about civil rights, I'd like to speak with you a little about what my childhood was like, growing up in the United States of America as a U.S. citizen, born of U.S. citizens. I'm from the South, and I grew up under what you might call the visible vestiges of slavery, the enforced inferiority of black people: separate school system, separate neighborhoods, separate cultural institutions, separated clubs, segregated jobs, segregated labor unions. Our lives were actually such that we never encountered white people except in highly structured circumstances. And the circumstances were always governed by a protocol that we had to learn. It was illegal for black people and white people to have social interaction with each other. I can remember several times when I was a teenager, I would be driving with some friends, we would be stopped by the police because somebody in the car, one of my friends, was very lightskinned, and the cops thought she was white. It's interesting to me now that all we had to do was to tell the white cop, "Oh, she's not white. She just looks like she's white." And that was an explanation. He said, "Okay." But I had to learn the protocol of racism. I couldn't cross the street because there were racial zoning laws. I could not enter a restroom unless it was marked "Colored Women." I could not imagine attending the University of Alabama, which was reserved for whites only.

But, of course, as we know, the civil rights movement successfully challenged racial segregation. When I go back to Birmingham now, I'm not encumbered by this protocol, by these zoning laws. I don't have to worry that there might not be a colored ladies' room; I can walk into any museum in the city; I can visit the main library downtown. I can be invited to speak at the University of Alabama, where I once would have been arrested if I tried to enter the campus.

But I would be grossly exaggerating the contemporary circumstances of my hometown, Birmingham, Alabama, if I generalized by saying that racism has been eliminated. Poverty is still concentrated in black communities. Schools in black communities are still substandard. Black people are still much less likely to attend college, especially the historically white institutions. And the numbers of black people behind bars are far greater today than anyone could have ever imagined during the civil rights era.

It's true that particular manifestations of racism, such as legal racial segregation, have been eliminated. But we have become so fixated on segregation as constituting the heart of racism that we cannot see the deep structural and institutional life of racism. Here we are, more than fifty years after the beginning of that civil rights movement, and we have people like Ward Connerly, and I don't even want to start talking about him. It seems that in the mid-twentieth century we understood the impact of racial segregation, first of all, because it was inscribed in the law. People could be arrested and sentenced to jail for violating the segregation statutes. Segregation was not only a system of separation, it was a system of surveillance that was supported by extralegal violence, by state violence. Of course, we know the names of some of the people who were executed or sentenced to death by the state, for example, the Scottsboro Nine; and we also know the names of some of the people who were victims of extralegal racist violence, like Emmett Till, Viola Liuzzo, and Schwerner, Goodman, and Chaney.

But the thing is, there are so many names we do not know. One of the things that happened when they were looking for Goodman, Chaney, and Schwerner was that they found other bodies, lots of them; the bodies of people who had never been looked for in a public manner, if at all. And I know that there are people currently working on the question of reparations, not in connection with slavery, but in connection with the crimes and injustices committed during the recent civil rights era.

The point I am trying to make is that we tend to think that racism was overt. Isn't that the word we use when we talk about segregation, when we talk about that era of legalized racism? Don't we tend to talk about it as being overt? And now we tend to think that it's hidden. I wonder why. Maybe it's because we have again learned not to notice it, because we have been persuaded that the only way to eliminate it is by pretending that it doesn't exist, that the only way to eliminate racism is to pretend that race doesn't exist. Therefore, we don't notice the dearth of black, Latino, Native American students on college campuses. If we ever enter a prison, it's not evident that we encounter a situation that is exactly the inverse of what we encounter on a university campus. In the segregated South, the signs of racism that were everywhere, the literal signs, made us pay notice to it. But now that the signs are gone, discriminatory practices continue under the sign of equality. So why do we not see the damage that racism is doing to our society? Why do we not see the damage that racist policies are doing to the world?

I'm not going to say racism is an equal-opportunity proposition here, but what I am going to say is that it does not necessarily coincide with the bodies of the people who are either explicitly or implicitly agents of racism. Look at our government. Look at Condoleezza Rice. Who could have imagined? When we were fighting for civil rights, who could have imagined that there would have been a black woman serving as the secretary of state of the United States of America, and then that's not all. It would have been hard for me to imagine that I could say in the twenty-first century, I would much prefer a white man to be secretary of state if he were opposed to racism and opposed to war.

One of the things I've said about Condoleezza is that, because we come from the same place, I'd notice these remarkable similarities in the way we narrated our own histories. And I said, how can this be? But then I realized that—I'll just summarize it—she narrates her story as a story of individual triumph. As a matter of fact, one of the things she said in an interview was that when she was growing up in Birmingham, everybody told her that in order to make it, a black person was going to have to run five times as fast as a white person in order to get the same thing. And she said, "But some of us ran eight times as fast." I would do a whole analysis of the uses of biography and all of that, but I think you get the point.

I wanted to say something about the civil rights movement and how the victories that we win are not always the victories that we thought we were fighting for. I don't think we should regret those struggles. Those struggles were absolutely important. But, of course, many of us thought we were changing the world. Many of us, if you move on from the civil rights movement and you talk about the liberation movements—the black liberation movement, the Chicano liberation movement, the Native American movements—we really thought that we were joining the revolutionary impulse that was happening around the world. There was Cuba, but also the liberation movements in Africa and in Latin America. Unfortunately, we didn't quite do that. A lot of us were persuaded that we were going to bring capitalism down, that we would have some kind of socialism. But we didn't.

But it doesn't mean that nothing has changed. A lot has changed. One of the things I've learned is that victories are never permanently engraved in the social landscape. What they mean at one point in history may be entirely different, and even contrary, to what they mean at another moment. We should be especially aware of how the notion of civil rights, especially for women and people of color, has been redefined in a way that contradicts its collective impact in favor of an individualized interpretation that pits individual white men against groups and classes that have suffered historical discrimination. (In so doing, we need to remember that white men are members of a class that has been a bearer of historical privilege, although not all white men have been privileged; there have been and continue to be plenty of white men who are poor.) But this doesn't mean that the struggle for affirmative action was a mistake, since it's now so often described as reverse discrimination. And even people who were the beneficiaries of affirmative action think of themselves as not deserving what they have. A lot of them are even ashamed to admit that they had a scholarship or a fellowship from an affirmative action program. Do you know what I mean?

Social meanings are always socially constructed, but we cannot leave it up to the state to produce these meanings, because we are always encouraged to conceptualize change only as it affects individuals. There is a dangerous individualism that is not unrelated to the possessive individualism of capitalism. And it is bound to transform the collective victories we win. If we imagine these victories as community victories and they are transformed into individual victories, then what happens is that we seek heroic examples, we seek individuals. There is a whole array of people like Gonzales, Thomas, and Rice. And then what happens is that we forget about the structural changes that were actually intended by those struggles.

I'll conclude by touching on the importance of the imagination and historical memory. Just as it was once important to imagine a world without slavery—and many people may have been thought insane for imagining a world without slavery, or imagining a world without segregation—we must challenge ourselves to imagine a world without prisons. When I was growing up in Birmingham, many people took racial segregation for granted without challenging themselves to imagine our society without it. A necessary step in winning greater freedom and greater justice is to imagine the world as we want it to be, a world in which women are not assumed to be inferior to men, a world without war, a world without xenophobia, a world without fenced borders designed to make us think of people from Mexico and Latin America as aliens and enemies. It is important to imagine a world in which binary conceptions of gender no longer govern modes of segregation or association, and one in which violence is eliminated from state practices as well as from our intimate lives, in heterosexual and same-sex relationships alike. And, of course, it is important to imagine a world without war.

This is just the beginning of a very long agenda for social change. If we are to fashion ourselves today into agents of social change, we will have to do a lot of work, a lot of work on ourselves, a lot of work with each other, and we have to try to make sense of what appears to be a really depressing world.

I think that we've learned how to respond to the feeling that what we are facing is just too much. It's tempting to say, nobody can do anything about it, let's just tune out and listen music on our iPods. What else do we do? Shop, play video games, watch TV? We have plenty of options when it comes to modes of distraction, but how many options are so clearly presented to us when it comes for getting involved? We have to figure out how to build community. I love music and I listen to my iPod all the time, so I'm really not criticizing anyone, but I want to feel that there is an enormous community of human beings who share a vision of the future. I want to know that we're committed to taking into account all the things we've learned over the last decades, the relationship between state violence and intimate violence. So let me just conclude now with a simple, final message that is really a plea. Please get involved. Please try to make a difference. Please try to turn this country, and the world, around.

EIGHT

The Meaning of Freedom

Metropolitan State College, Denver
February 15, 2008

Since the theme of this conference acknowledges the two hundreth anniversary of the abolition of the slave trade in 1808, I decided to talk about the meaning of freedom. The conference theme emphasizes two hundred years of freedom. What has that freedom meant for people of African descent? What has that freedom meant for the black world? And what has been the relationship to communities that are differently racialized but which, nonetheless, suffer under cycles of oppression?

I suppose that very few people think about the fact that the institution of the prison has claimed a place at the very core of black history, particularly since the abolition of slavery. It has been a constant theme in the collective lives of black people in this country. It has also been a constant theme in the collective lives of Chicanos. And it is increasingly a major aspect of the lives of people who are racially oppressed in Europe, as well as in Latin America, and when one looks at the continent of Africa, one can readily see the extent to which the institution of the prison is actually beginning to replace institutions like education and health care.

When Carter G. Woodson proposed in 1926 that the nation annually set aside one week for the celebration of Negro

History Week, he was confronting a dominant culture that almost totally marginalized black accomplishments, and it was important to transmit the message that we were capable of vastly more than white-supremacist society attributed to black communities.

Then, of course, a half-century later the celebration was extended to the entire month. The month of February offers us a kind of microcosm of the history of the black world. February is the month, as far as the United States of America is concerned, when the Fifteenth Amendment authorized black male suffrage.

February is significant to black history of many other reasons as well. The Freemen's Aid Society was founded in February. W. E. B. DuBois was born on February 23, 1868, and it was on February 23, 1972, that I was released on bail. But it was also during the month of February that W. E. B. DuBois convened the first Pan-African Congress in 1919 to urge people of African descent throughout the world to unite in order to stand up against European imperialism. February was also the month when the Southern Christian Leadership Conference, Martin Luther King's organization, was established, and when the students staged sit-ins at the lunch counters in Greensboro, North Carolina. That was in February of 1960. We could actually continue to do a whole panorama of black history by looking at key events that happened during the month of February.

What I'd like to say now is that Black History Month seems to have become an occasion to generate profit. If you look at the Walmart Web site, Walmart, which is the largest corporation in the world, you will see how they urge you to celebrate black history by buying their products. Wal-Mart, as the largest corporation in the world, demonstrates the impact that global capitalism has had on our lives and the conditions of neoliberalism under which we live and think. Through Walmart's action we see how capitalism has insinuated itself into our desires, our dreams, and our ways of thinking about ourselves. We commodify ourselves when we talk about how we're going to market ourselves. So keep that in mind as we go back and look at some aspects of black history.

We most frequently celebrate Black History Month by evoking a collection of narratives about individual black people who managed to overcome the barriers created by the racism of the past, whereas we should have a broader conception of what it means to celebrate the legacies of black history, and those legacies should not be confined simply to people of African descent. I'm thinking of someone like Yuri Kochiyama, who is a Japanese American woman who has for the overwhelming majority of her life—and she's about 82 years old now—worked in the civil rights movement, worked to free political prisoners. She was with Malcolm X when he was assassinated, and there is a picture of her cradling Malcolm X's head in her hands as he lay dying. We don't necessarily bring Yuri Kochiyama into our celebrations of Black History Month. Or Elizabeth "Betita" Martínez, who was one of the most amazing activists in the early civil rights movement.

We celebrate individuals, but we also evoke the legislative and court victories that have helped to produce a black subject that putatively enjoys equality before the law. Therefore, we rightly celebrate the abolition of the slave trade in 1808, and we also celebrate the Thirteenth Amendment that we think abolished slavery, and we celebrate the Civil Rights Act of 1964, which one of the candidates insisted could only be the work of a president, and the Voting Rights Act of 1965. Many of these legislative moments were attempts to confront and eradicate the vestiges of slavery.

I think that all of us, regardless of our racial or ethnic background, feel relieved that we no longer have to deal with the racism and the sexism associated with the system of slavery. But we treat the history of enslavement like we treat the genocidal colonization of indigenous people in North America, as if it was not that important, or worse, as if never really happened. We think of it as a kind of nightmare. And, as is often the case with nightmares, we try not to think about it except in abstract terms, and we assume that it will go away. One of the amazing contributions of a group of black women writers, beginning, say, in the 1980s, was to think about slavery and to imagine the subjectivities of persons who were enslaved and not allow us to continue to think in these abstract categories.

The institution of the prison tells us that the nightmare of slavery continues to haunt us. If we actually learn how to recognize the forms of racism and sexism that are at the structural core of the prison system, that means we'll have to develop a very different idea about the state of democracy in the United States of America, particularly with respect to its victories over racism and sexism. We hear the Bush administration constantly evoking the civil rights movement as the completion of democracy in the United States, American democracy.

The theme of this gathering is how to end cycles of oppression. I want to talk about that by making the connection between slavery and the contemporary prison system. First I want to say that the emancipation that awaited enslaved people in 1863, people whose history under slavery had been primarily a history of striving for freedom, was a constrained emancipation. The joyful noise of freedom to which W. E. B. DuBois refers in *Black Reconstruction* had to fend off the forms of unfreedom that were tenaciously clinging to the emancipation offered to the slaves. What did it mean to be a former slave who was free? What did that freedom mean? DuBois talks about the spectacular dimensions of this newfound freedom, and there were spectacular dimensions, because black people for the first time had the freedom to learn, the freedom to try to get an education, the freedom to create schools, with what meager resources were there, the freedom to travel for the first time. But, of course, this was a gendered freedom, because it was mostly black men who were able to take advantage of the freedom to travel.

They also had the sexual freedom to choose their own sexual partners, which we might minimize today, but considering that there were so many other dimensions of freedom that were not available to the enslaved people who had been "set free," that sexual freedom became so important that it becomes the major theme of the first popular music to be produced in the aftermath of slavery: the blues.

Sexual freedom then becomes a metaphor for other kinds of freedom, for political freedom, for economic freedom. But these forms of freedom were shrouded in unfreedom. The enslavers whose activity was abolished by the Emancipation Proclamation, and then later by amendment to the Constitution, did not surrender so easily to words. It strikes me to be very strange that over the decades we have assumed that it was possible to abolish slavery simply by proclamation, a few words here, and by a clause in the Constitution, when that proclamation and that constitutional amendment never clearly explain how they understand slavery.

So we don't even clearly know what was supposed to be abolished. Was it chattel slavery? Was it treating human beings as property? Human beings are still bought and sold and still treated as property, including people like Shaquille O'Neal, who just got traded, right? Was it about coerced labor? We know there is so much coerced labor, and we look at ways in which undocumented immigrants are treated and we see a very similar mode of labor. As a result, I don't think that the U.S. Constitution successfully abolished coercive labor. What about the whole scaffolding of racist ideology that was necessary to keep an entire people enslaved? Did that get abolished? So why do we assume that slavery was abolished?

Slavery was a part of the warp and woof of American life, especially in the South, but also in the North. And words alone were not sufficient to make it go away. If slavery was declared dead, it was simultaneously reincarnated through new institutions, new practices, new ideologies. We can think about the ways in which the institutions of punishment have served as receptacles for these structures and ideologies of enslavement that were translated into the terms of freedom—slavery translated into the terms of freedom. What have these generations of "freedom" meant since the passage of the Thirteenth Amendment? Both the prison and the fate of former slaves would be inextricably linked to the struggle for democracy in this country. So when we talk about the relationship between slavery and the prison, we're also talking about the nature of democracy, or what goes under the rubric of democracy in this country.

Prison continues to reflect the closure of the doors of democracy to major sectors of the U.S. population. We can say that one of the major aspects of slavery was social death. That also included civil death. That meant that slaves could not participate in the political arena or in civil life. So what about felon disenfranchisement today? What about the fact that there are 2.2 million people behind bars on any given day? Statistics can be deceptive. Many of us know that figure, 2.2 million, but that only reflects a census survey: It's the average number of people who are in prison on any given day. If you look at the number of people who go in and out of the prison and jail system over the course of a year, that's going to be approximately 13 million people. So that's much more vast than we have the habit of thinking about.

The vast majority of these millions of people come from communities of color. This has to do with the increasingly restrictive and repressive nature of U.S. society. There is a majority of black people in prison throughout the country, but if you look at my state, California, the majority of people in California are Latinos and Chicanos.

The Structural Racism of the Prison

What's very interesting is that people don't get convicted anymore because they are black or because they are Chicano. But there are structures of racism that makes race matter in terms of determining who goes to prison, particularly who gets to go to prison and who gets to go to colleges and universities. How can we think about that structural racism? What is the relationship between the structural racism of slavery and the racism that is inscribed in the very processes that create trajectories that lead inevitably toward incarceration or higher education?

The structural racism of the prison can also be held responsible for the persistence of racism in the so-called free world. We are encouraged to think about racial equality as produced by adopting postures of color-blindness, right? We are told that all we have to do is not notice race and racism is going to leave, it will go away. So there is a kind of learned ignorance, because we can see race, but we know we are *not supposed to* see race. There is a kind of repression that oftentimes produces these many explosive expressions of racism. I can remember Michael Richards saying, "I'm not a racist. I don't even know where that came from." Increasingly, this is what people say. They can't understand how it is that a racist observation escapes from their lips. There is a whole psychic reservoir of racism in this country. It's in the structures, it's in our collective psyche. All of us are affected by it. I'm not only talking about white people as the bearers of racism. I'm talking about ideologies and logics that inform the way all of us relate to the world.

Prisons, of course, thrive on class inequalities, they thrive on racial inequalities, they thrive on gender inequalities. They produce and reproduce those inequalities, because they segregate and isolate the individuals they punish. They also conceal the inequalities that they reproduce. The hidden danger of relying on incarceration as the major solution to behaviors that are often the by-products of poverty is that the solution reproduces the very problem it purports to solve. This is how we might begin to understand why the prison population constantly rises, not only in absolute numbers, but proportionately as well. It has nothing to do with the rise in crime statistics. As the rate of crime goes down, prison populations go up.

Of course, they reproduce these problems because funds almost inevitably migrate away from education and housing and health care toward what they call corrections. Therefore, one generation spawns another. The crime rate has fallen, but the incarceration rate has risen. In the United States, of course, a prison sentence on a felony charge is a life sentence, regardless of how many years one gets. It is a life sentence because of what someone like Marc Mauer calls "collateral consequences"—the collateral consequences of imprisonment that lead to social death, disenfranchisement. We wouldn't have had to deal with the Bush administration over the last seven years had it not been for the case that due to felony disenfranchisement more than 600,000 people could not vote in Florida. In the 2000 elections there was only a 537-vote difference. So if a tiny minority of those 600,000 had been able to vote, we might have had an entirely different course of history.

If the prison is proposed as a solution to social issues, then other possibilities get excluded. Governor Schwarzenegger, the governor of the state in which I live, changed the name of the California Department of Corrections to the California Department of Rehabilitation and Corrections. If we really want rehabilitation, then we have to start talking about decarceration. How is rehabilitation possible under conditions of total confinement? How is rehabilitation possible when there is no way that people can exercise their freedoms? As a matter of fact, that's the whole point of the punishment as imprisonment: It deprives you of your rights and liberties. That is why the prison is a peculiarly democratic punishment. It is the quintessential democratic institution, because it provides you with the negation of that upon which the whole concept of bourgeois democracy has been developed.

In our society, the assumption is that if you are from a certain racialized community, you will have had some contact with the prison system. There was an interesting study that was conducted by a sociologist who matched black and white pairs of job applicants. Some of them indicated that they had a criminal conviction and some of them didn't. What was very interesting was that white people who had a felony conviction were called back for interviews at the same rate as black people who had the same credentials but had no criminal record. The point that Marc Mauer makes is that black men are essentially born with the social stigma equivalent to a felony conviction. So we're talking about an institution that not only affects those it incarcerates; it has an influence on entire communities.

The problem is not limited to black men. Women constitute, and have constituted for a while, the fasting-growing sector of the imprisoned population. And women of color, of course, constitute the largest group of women, therefore the fastest-growing population within the entire imprisoned population. This is not just the case in the United States. It's true in Canada, it's increasingly true in Europe, and it's true in other countries as well.

If we look at who is in prison and why they are there, then it's clear that race and class have much more to do with the overcrowding of these prison institutions than the existence of crime. Once people have spent time in prison, they are forever haunted by their status as prisoners. They are forever haunted by civil death. They are forever excluded from certain aspects of democratic participation in the society. So this is a way of understanding why black and Latino people are so easily labeled criminal, so easily identified as threats to law and order, and it helps us understand why people from those communities often see their own sisters and brothers as the criminals, as the menaces and threats. The immigrant, for example, is scapegoated. The undocumented immigrant is seen as the enemy.

And there is a racialization of immigration. The post-colonial, post-Soviet, post-socialist immigration to this country involves people arriving here from all over the world, especially from Russia. But do we ever think about undocumented immigrants as Russian? Do we ever racialize them as white? So we begin to understand how the ideology of racism really infects the very logic of our thought and our relations to one another.

I want to talk for a moment about how this criminalization process, particularly with respect to black people, is anchored in slavery. And I want to make a connection between the democracy we think we now enjoy and the democracy that was offered to people of African descent in the aftermath of slavery. Even during slavery there was a contradiction in the way black people were thought about. We tend to think slavery meant that black people were treated as property, right? That's chattel slavery. But then black people were punished, they were found guilty of crime. Can property be accountable? Can property be found culpable? There was something wrong there. As a matter of fact, you can say that even though black people were not acknowledged as having legal personality in most senses, when they committed a crime, they were accountable to the law, and therefore they were acknowledged as having legal personality.

This negative affirmation of the legal personality of black people continues to hold sway today. You might say that the proof of participation of black people in U.S. democracy is precisely the fact that they have received due process before being sentenced in such disproportionate numbers to prison. It is precisely as they appear before the law as equal subjects who get due process, precisely because they are considered accountable, or it's through their culpability—does that make sense?—through their culpability that they participate in the democratic process. That reflects the contradiction of slavery, and that, I think, is an indication of one of the ways in which slavery continues to haunt us.

Before I complete my presentation I have to say something about corporate globalization. I have to say that corporate globalization has become the major threat to democracy in the world. But the problem is that capitalism represents itself as synonymous with democracy. That is what George Bush is talking about when he calls for the defense of democracy against terror. That is the democracy that the U.S. military is fighting to protect in places like Iraq and Afghanistan. It's not democracy, it's capitalism, or it's a democracy that uses capitalism as its model, that sees the free market as the paradigm for freedom and that sees competition as the paradigm for freedom.

Corporations are linked to the global marketing of imprisonment. They reap enormous profits in this area—prisons at the expense of housing and health care and education and other social services. As a matter of fact, the neoliberal conception of economic freedom requires the government to withdraw from virtually all social services. The market is supposed to determine everything. Freedom emerges because the market will determine the distribution of education, the distribution of health care. And according to the Chicago boys, Milton Friedman and those people, it will even itself out. I guess they still believe in Adam Smith's "invisible hand," that somehow or another freedom will reveal itself.

But when we look at the extent to which countries in the southern region have been devastated by the juggernaut of privatization, a country like South Africa, which is still, I suppose, our hope for a non-racist and non-sexist and non-homophobic society, they're experiencing enormous problems precisely as a result of privatization that is required by the IMF and other international financial organizations as that which countries must do who wish to get international loans. It's really scary.

We see that kind of structural adjustment happen in this country. That is why we are confronted with this crisis of health care and why health care has become totally privatized since the 1980s. There was an attempt to totally privatize the prison system as well. It worked in some places; it didn't quite work in others. But we see the insinuation of private corporations into the prison system all over this country.

I wonder why we do not find it utterly shameful that it is possible now to visit countries in the global South and discover that while their educational systems and housing subsidies and jobs have deteriorated over the last quarter-century under the impact of globalization, it is often possible to discover a shiny new prison that would lead one to believe that one had been teleported back to Colorado or California. Of course, we use the term "prison-industrial complex" to point out that there is this global proliferation of prisons and prisoners that is more clearly linked to economic and political structures and ideologies than to individual criminal conduct and efforts to curb crime.

I wanted to say a few words about this prison-industrial complex that has this increasingly privileged place within the global economy and the way in which it serves to support the persistence of racism, but also how it has become a gendering apparatus. I don't think we think about the fact that there are prisons for men and there are prisons for women. What about people who are gender-nonconforming? Because I think we've learned over the last period that there are more than two genders. So what happens to them? Where do they go? Where does a transgender woman get sent or a transgender man get sent or someone who doesn't necessarily identify as male or female? Of course, the prisons rely on the old notions of biology, that biology has the answers for everything, so they inspect people's genitals. It's based on the genitalia that they get classified as a certain gender and therefore sent to certain prisons.

Then, of course, there are problems with violence. People often argue, well, if you send a transgendered woman to men's prisons because she has male genitalia, she's going to be subject to rape, because we know, we think, that rape is something that male prisoners begin to do once they go to prison. We don't ask ourselves why, where does that come from? We don't ask ourselves about the extent to which the institution itself promotes that violence, needs that violence, generates that sexual violence in order for the system to work. Then we see it happen in Abu Ghraib and we see it happen in Guantánamo, and we express such shock—this is not the way America is supposed to operate. However, if we look at what happens on a daily basis in the domestic prisons in this country, we see similar coercion and violence.

Of course, women have been especially hurt by these developments. The prison industrial complex has brought in women from the global South, indigenous women in disproportionate numbers. If you go to Australia, who do you think you will discover in disproportionate numbers in the prisons there, in the women's prisons especially?

The prison-industrial complex has become so big and powerful that it works to perpetuate itself. It's literally self-perpetuating. The raw materials are immigrant youth and youth of color throughout the world. So if one visits a prison in Australia or France, the Netherlands, Italy, Sweden, one sees young people who come from communities that we in the United States designate as communities of color, we see indigenous people. Race continues to matters a great deal throughout the world today.

This is something that the United States has basically offered to the world: a way of managing social problems by refusing to confront them. Instead of solving issues, the system puts people behind bars. We can't deny that there are people in prison who have done horrible, hurtful things to others. But these aren't the majority of prisoners. And there are many people in the free world who have done horrible, hurtful things. There are many reasons why people engage in violence, sometimes out of malice, sometimes out of mental illness, sometimes out of self-defense. Many women who are in prison for committing violent acts have killed in desperation in order to extricate themselves from a violent intimate relationship. No matter what a person has been convicted of, does it make sense to house hundreds, sometimes thousands of people together, or separately in isolation cells, deprive them of contact with their families, deprive them of education, and then assume that this is going to help rehabilitate them and help them be a healthy part of society?

I'd like to end with questions. How do we imagine and struggle for a democracy that does not spawn forms of terror, that does not spawn war, that does not need enemies for its sustenance? Because people who are in prison are pointed to as the enemies of society, and that is one of the ways in which we can define our own sense of ourselves as free, by looking at those who are our opposites. How do we imagine a democracy that does not thrive on this racism, that does not thrive on homophobia, that is not based on the rights of capitalist corporations to plunder the world's economic and social and physical environments?

I suggest we use our imaginations to try to come up with versions of democracy in which, for example, the practice of Islam does not serve as a pretext for incarceration in an immigration detention facility or in a military prison, where torture and sexual coercion are not considered appropriate treatment. We need to use our imaginations to envision versions of democracy that allow for many things: the right to decent, fulfilling employment and a living wage; the right to quality education; the right to live in a world where education is not a commodity, but rather a creative discipline that allows us to understand all the worlds we inhabit, both human and nonhuman, the kind of education that compels us to transcend the limits of nationalist patriotism in order to imagine ourselves as citizens of the globe.

Question from the Audience

What is your opinion about the presidential election and Obama?

I am not a Democrat, and I've never actually been a registered member of either of the two major parties. I've been a registered member of the Communist Party, I've been a registered member of the Peace and Freedom Party, and now I'm registered Green. During these primaries, I voted for Cynthia McKinney, because I'm a Green Party member. I found that it's very interesting that the media has completely blocked out coverage of the independent parties; they ignore political parties that are not either Republican or Democrat.

What do I think about the elections? I think that it's absolutely amazing that there is so much interest. It's a really exciting moment in this country; it's particularly exciting to see young people—who have been described as apathetic—get deeply involved. We are generations of apathetic voters, so they tell us. We come to find out that people were apathetic because there was no one interesting to vote for or to support.

But I'm always very cautious when it comes to electoral politics. I think that particularly here in this country we have a tendency to invest our own collective power in individuals. We have what I sometimes call a messiah complex. This is why, when we think of the civil rights movement, we think of Martin Luther King. We can't imagine that that movement could have been created by huge numbers of people whose names we do not even know. We can't imagine that.

I often emphasize that the Montgomery bus boycott, which for many people is a defining moment of the civil rights movement, would not have been possible had it not been for black women domestic workers. These are the people we never think about. They are totally invisible, invisible in history, but those are the women who refused to ride the bus. Those are the black people who were riding the bus because they were riding from black communities to white communities, because they were cleaning white people's houses and cooking white people's food and doing their laundry. But we can't imagine that they were the agents of history that gave us this amazing civil rights movement.

All of which is to say this enthusiasm, this incredible enthusiasm that's been generated over the last period that has been called a movement—and Obama has specifically referred to what's happening around his campaign as a movement—if it is to be a movement, it has to demand much more than the election of a single individual, no matter what that individual may represent. I think in a sense Obama is a canvas onto which many of us are painting our desires and our dreams and our hopes. That might be okay if we understand that that's what we're doing, and if we understand that it's not enough to do that, and if we understand that even if he is elected, or if Hillary is, if either one of them is elected, we have to keep up the pressure, because we can't expect them to do all of the work that we should be doing for ourselves.

NINE

Justice for Lesbian, Gay, Bisexual, and Transgender Communities

Midwest Bisexual Lesbian Gay Transgender Ally College Conference
University of Illinois, Urbana-Champaign
February 24, 2008

I thank the organizers of the Midwest Bisexual Lesbian Gay Transgender Ally College Conference for having invited me to deliver the closing keynote.

I arrived yesterday in time to meet with some of the conference organizers—Oliver, the keynote chair; Sara Clemons, who introduced me; and Treva. I have run into people in the elevators, from Grinnell College, for example. I also attended the Las Crudas concert, and I was clearly oldest person there.

I understand that the theme of your conference this year is "Voting for Change: Liberty and Justice for All." Given the debate within the context of the current election campaign on the meaning of change in the aftermath of eight years of the Bush administration, this is a very fitting theme.

But I fear that the last seven and a half years have so stunned us that even relatively imperceptible changes seem to have huge consequences. Let us not sell ourselves short. I've heard many comments about the intelligence of the candidates in both parties. Not that they aren't all intelligent, and not to disparage any one of these individuals, but to tell the truth, compared to George W. Bush, almost anyone would appear to be "very intelligent."

As we face all the problems in our lives and in the world, from the so-called global war on terror to the many manifestations of racism, both subtle and violent, to attacks on lesbian, gay, bisexual, and transgender communities, to attacks on our rights to education and the denial of health care to increasing numbers of people, we acknowledge all these problems, we need hope, we need imagination, we need communities of struggle, we need to realize that change is indeed possible.

How do we know that change is possible? It is possible because, as horrendous as things might seem today, we are living in a world that has been shaped by change. As difficult as conditions are for poor people of color in this country, they would certainly be worse if ordinary people had not learned how to identify with communities of struggle, had not learned how to imagine a different and better world.

As difficult as conditions are for young lesbian, gay, bisexual, and transgender people—and sometime one's sexual or gender identification can be a matter of life and death—still, over the last thirty to forty years, courageous advocates for LGBT rights have led us in the direction of a better world.

The point is, people have massively and collectively organized for change, and the world we live in today, however many problems remain, is the result of those movements.

I think about my own past as an activist and my involvement in communities of young people who truly believed that we could end war and racism. I sometimes wonder whether we who struggled so urgently for peace and justice and better worlds could have ever predicted that four decades later we would be confronting an even more ferocious war machine. Could we have predicted the globalization of poverty and racism with which we now live? Could we have foreseen the transmutation of the rhetorics and violences of anti-communism into global war under the pretext of conquering terrorism?

Could we have foreseen the emergence of a violent neo-conservatism that thrives on white supremacy, patriarchy, xenophobia, Islamophobia, and heterosexism? Probably not. But one thing is certain: if past struggles had not stood up, spoken out, committed civil disobedience, fought, and exerted their influence to reshape human affairs, our world would be more materially and spiritually impoverished, and we would certainly not be able to carry on today. Student movements, civil rights movements, anti-war movements, women's movements, gay and lesbian movements, solidarity movements with national liberation struggles in Africa, Asia, the Middle East, Latin America have all contributed immeasurably to making our world a more just one.

As disheartening as our contemporary circumstances might appear, let us all acknowledge that things could have gotten a lot worse than they are. What is more, if it were not for all the mass struggles of the past, we might not even have the force of imagination to apprehend that our collective action can indeed bring about radical change. And I see your generation picking up a new banner and moving us forward.

We are living in a world that did not have to come to this. The war in Iraq did not have to happen. George Bush did not have to be elected—*he was not elected!*

What would the world look like today, what would be the prospects for democracy, if ex-prisoners had been able to vote in the 2000 elections?

Voting is an important civil right. But I fear that if our progressive political energy is so narrowly focused on the elections, we may forget that there are other forms of collective political intervention. So, while we absolutely need to accelerate our involvement in the voting process—and we can, indeed, vote for change—voting for change is only the beginning. Participation in the elections at all levels needs to be complemented by ongoing involvement in social movements, and by focusing not only on specifically LGBT issues, but on anti-racist and anti-sexist activism, on immigrants' rights, on anti-war activism, on prisoners' rights, against privatization, for labor rights, for environmental justice, etc., and also by learning how to recognize and formulate the deep connections among all these issues.

So voting for change ought to be complemented by advocating and organizing for change—for radical change.

I don't want to appear to underestimate the power of the vote, especially since legislative strategies have been pivotal to the quest for justice for LGBT communities. However, even as we desperately need those remedies and protections that can be guaranteed by law, we cannot depend on the law alone as a solution to the problem of homophobia.

In Oxnard, California, a little under two weeks ago a 15-year old boy by the name of Lawrence King was killed by a classmate after he had publicly come out at his junior high school. He had been bullied by a group of boys after he started wearing high-heeled shoes and lipstick to school. The boy who killed him was only 14 years old. Apparently, he walked into the school's computer lab where Lawrence King was studying and shot him in the head.

This tragedy has so many dimensions beyond the horrendous and unnecessary death of a young boy. According to the *New York Times*, he was living in a group home for abused foster children.

The 14-year-old boy who killed him will be tried as an adult—as if he possessed the individual agency to decide for himself that homosexual and transgender people are so repulsive that they do not deserve to live. Where did he get this idea from?

The attribution of absolute guilt to the individual in this case is the same logic that allowed the U.S. government and U.S. military to shift responsibility for the horrendous sexual tortures in Abu Ghraib onto a few individuals, "a few bad apples."

In the case of Lawrence King, the killer will be tried for a hate crime and if he is convicted, he will spend from fifty-two years to life in prison. This boy will be the scapegoat for a heteronormative society and a government that is deeply homophobic, and that homophobia will continue.

Moreover, if we rely on the prison system to solve the problem of homophobia, we are relying on a system that is complicit in the process that has rendered homophobia socially acceptable.

If we rely on the institution of the prison as the primary mode of addressing the social problems that lead people to prison, then these problems will continue to thrive, and they will continue to be reproduced by the prison. The prison is one of society's major institutional gendering apparatuses, and encourages and relies on homophobia.

I understand that the name of Martin Luther King has been evoked on several occasions during this conference. This is Black History Month; I am troubled that our popular historical memory has become so superficial that the name of Martin Luther King has come to stand in for a history that is far more complicated than his dream. The popularization of Martin

Luther King has further contributed to this country's historical amnesia.

One of Martin Luther King's most trusted advisers, the man who introduced King to the Gandhian concept of non-violent resistance, the man who was a major organizer of the 1963 March on Washington, was Bayard Rustin, a black man who was openly gay before the emergence of the gay liberation movement. Bayard Rustin had also been a member of the Communist Party.

Rustin was attacked by Senator Strom Thurmond as a "Communist, draft-dodger, and homosexual." Although Dr. King was consistent and principled in his support of Bayard Rustin, other leaders, including Roy Wilkins, the chair of the NAACP at that time, refused to allow Rustin to take credit for the work he did in organizing what remains the most well-known historical demonstration in Washington. This was the march where Dr. King gave his "I Have a Dream" speech.

Two years later, in March 1965, Dr. King published an article in the *New York Times Magazine* under the title "Civil Right #1: The Right to Vote." The next day President Lyndon Johnson delivered an address on the Voting Rights Bill, which was passed on August 6.

This must be one of the moments Hillary Clinton was referring to when she said that it took a president to realize Dr. King's ideals.

First of all, the civil rights movement was about far more than a single leader. Thousands and thousands of anonymous people learned how to imagine a radically changed world. King gave expression to their aspirations, and people like Bayard Rustin helped to translate these aspirations into a movement. This is the history that is erased by the reduction of the civil rights movement to one name: Martin Luther King.

Perhaps Clinton is implicitly comparing Obama to Dr. King; obviously he has listened very carefully to King's speeches, and she to Johnson.

Why has neither political party spent much time discussing the contemporary state of civil rights? Will either of them insist on the inclusion of transgender people?

There is a direct link between the historical struggles for civil rights for people of African descent in this country and the contemporary struggles for civil rights for LGBT communities. This means that we need to speak out against the efforts of black evangelicals who refuse to acknowledge the connections between historical struggles for civil rights for black people and current struggles for the civil rights of LGBT communities.

If we take civil rights seriously, we cannot argue that the civil rights movement is over, that this is the post–civil rights era or the post-race era. Huge numbers of people cannot exercise their civil rights and are exiled to the margins of the polity. LGBT communities do not enjoy the full protections of civil rights. Immigrant communities, especially undocumented immigrants, have been refused the protections of civil rights. Millions of prisoners and former prisoners are denied their civil rights.

Except for those in Maine and Vermont, people in prisons cannot vote. Ex-felons cannot vote in many states. Felon disenfranchisement is one major reason why Bush emerged victorious in the 2000 elections.

I do not want to underestimate the importance of civil rights, the rights of citizenship. But in this country, the rights of citizenship are construed in a very narrow and formalistic way. In the United States, rights tend to be separated from access to the resources that we might need to take advantage of those rights. The right to be free of discrimination on the job—which is still not guaranteed to LGBT communities—has been delinked from the right to a job in the first place. Housing discrimination, but not the right to affordable housing. Health care, but not the right to free health care. Education, but not the right to free education.

Four decades ago, a debate developed between Martin Luther King and Malcolm X around the questions of civil rights and human rights. A bizarre legal situation emerged during the civil rights struggle: civil rights activists were murdered, but Southern states refused to prosecute their murders. The only path to prosecution—federal civil rights law.

Forty years ago, Malcolm argued that we expand our perspective from civil rights to human rights. But we have still not developed a discourse that allows us to identify and build movements against the extensive human rights violations committed in this country. Thus, torture is not a human rights violation; the murder of Lawrence King is not a human rights violation.

Now, I want to look briefly at two of the most salient civil rights issues that have mobilized LGBT communities and allies. The first is the case of equality in marriage, and the second is the case of equality in the military.

In reflecting on the formal argument regarding gender and sexual equality in the military, we should ask ourselves why we are inclined to rely on abstract logic—equality as equal access, equal access of people of color to the military, equal access of women to combat, equal access of gays and lesbians to the military.

While I would never suggest that these struggles around formal equality are not important, it is equally important to consider that to which underrepresented groups demand access. I would think that such "democratic" demands would also have to consider the deeply anti-democratic nature of the institution. Equality would be best served by the equal right to refuse military service—for white men, white women, women and men of color, and gays and lesbians of all racial and ethnic backgrounds.

The debates around gay marriage require a more complicated approach. The structures of heteronormativity, and the various violences these structures and discourses entail, do not necessarily disappear when the sexuality of the participants is changed. I'm not suggesting that we do not claim the right of gays and lesbians to engage in this practice, but we also have to think about the institution itself. It is an economic institution. It is about property. It is not about human relations, or intimate relations.

What does it mean to demand the equal right to marriage without recognizing the role that marriage has played in the reproduction of race and gender inequalities? Under conditions of bourgeois democracy, marriage has always been a sexist, racist, and heterosexist institution that is primarily about the accumulation and distribution of property.

Enslaved people were not allowed to marry, and when configurations of family developed that did not correspond to the nuclear family, complex racist ideologies were spawned to further consolidate racist hierarchies. We live with those ideologies today. During George Bush's campaign for marriage, deep structural problems related to racism were attributed to the absent father. As if all single mothers need to do is marry and they will transcend the conditions of poverty in which they are ensconced. And they must marry a man, even if that man is unemployed.

Even within LGBT communities, we discover the influence of poisonous racist ideologies.

I draw an example from the work of the Fairness Campaign in Louisville, Kentucky. The Fairness Campaign describes its core values as follows:

1. We believe gay, lesbian, bisexual, and transgender people have the right to respect, dignity, and full equality.
2. We believe that dismantling racism is central to our work.
3. We believe that all issues of oppression are linked and can only be addressed by working in coalition.
4. We believe in non-violent grassroots organizing that empowers individuals and builds a social movement that creates lasting change.

Thus, they publicly spoke out against the performance of a gay white man during the last Derby in a local nightclub. This man, Chuck Knipp, dressed up in blackface and women's clothes to portray a black welfare mother called Shirley Q. Liquor with nineteen children whose names were malt liquor brands and venereal diseases. As it turns out, the Fairness supporters were criticized by some people as not being "gay" enough. After all, it was all in jest.

If Don Imus and Michael Richards and Kelly Tilghman are publicly criticized for their racist comments, then shouldn't there be an even more passionate resistance to such racist humor when it happens under the cover of gay popular culture?

There is much more to say, but I thought I would conclude by sharing with you a poem titled "Where Do You Go to Be a Non-Citizen?" that was quite popular in queer of color circles in the 1980s in the San Francisco Bay Area. It was written by black, feminist, lesbian poet Pat Parker, who died in 1989, and is included in her collection *Movement in Black*.

Because most of you were not born when she wrote this poem, you probably will not understand the historical references. But this does not mean that she and her feminist, intersectional, crosscutting approach should not be a part of your historical memory.

In Pat Parker's poem, there are eerie resonances with the contemporary period. I'm thinking about her question "where do you go to be a non-citizen?"—which is a question that to-day speaks solidarity with undocumented people. I'm thinking about her references to Taft College and Carmel, which today evokes the Jena Six, and I am thinking about the New Jersey Four. If Pat were still living she would make sure that everybody understood the connections between the racist assault on the Jena Six, and the racist/heterosexist assault on the young black lesbians who tried to defend themselves in New York's Greenwich Village and the homophobic murder of Lawrence King.

Where do you go to become a non-citizen?

I want to resign; I want out.
I want to march to the nearest place
Give my letter to a smiling face
I want to resign; I want out.

President Ford vetoed a jobs bill
Sent to him from capital hill
While we sit by being super cool
He gets a $60,000 swimming pool
I wanna resign; I want out.

$68,000 to Queen Elizabeth to not grow cotton.
Yet there's no uproar that this jive is rotten
$14,000 to Ford Motors to not plant wheat

I guess the government don't want wheat all over the seats.
I wanna resign; I want out

The CIA Commission was in session for 26 weeks long
Said the boys didn't do too much wrong
They gave out acid—a test—so they tell
Yet, if you and I used it—we'd be in jail
I wanna resign; I want out.

And from Taft College—a small group of fools
Chased all the Black students out of the school.
And good citizens worried about property sale
Chased away Black teenagers from picturesque Carmel.
I wanna resign; I want out.

The little league after using all excuses up
Says a 10 year old girl must use a boys supportive cup
An International Women's Congress in Mexico to make plans
Elected for their president—a white liberal man
I wanna resign; I want out.

The A.P.A. finally said all gays aren't ill
Yet ain't no refunds on their psychiatry bills
A federal judge says MCC is valid—a reality
Yet it won't keep the pigs from hurting you or me
I wanna resign; I want out

I wanna resign; I want out
Please lead me to the place
Show me the smiling face
I'm skeptical—full of doubt
I wanna resign; I want out.

TEN

Recognizing Racism in the Era of Neoliberalism

Vice Chancellor's Oration on the Elimination of Racial
*   Discrimination*
Murdoch University, Perth, Western Australia
March 18, 2008

On March 21, 1960, South African police killed sixty-nine peaceful demonstrators in the township of Sharpeville. I am honored to have been invited to deliver the Vice-Chancellor's Oration on the occasion of the International Day for the Elimination of Racial Discrimination, which honors the Sharpeville martyrs. I am particularly honored to be here in Australia in the aftermath of the first apology by a head of state to the indigenous people of this country, and I would like to acknowledge the traditional owners of this land.

On February 1, 1960, less than two months before the Sharpeville Massacre in South Africa, in the U.S. city of Greensboro, North Carolina, black students sat down at a Woolworth's lunch counter. Traditionally, black people were only served if they remained standing. This sit-in became a catalyst for an important moment in the U.S. civil rights movement. I vividly remember that day, for as a black person in the United States, I had grown up in Birmingham, Alabama, which in the 1950s was known as the most racially segregated city in our country. I had stood up many times at the Woolworth's lunch counter in my city, experiencing the humiliation of being treated as not sufficiently human to be able to sit down and eat a sandwich.

As a child I had first discovered South African apartheid when I learned that Birmingham, Alabama, my hometown, was known as the Johannesburg of the South. Indeed, the regime of white supremacy that influenced every aspect of our lives relied, as did South African apartheid, on the notion that social order required absolute racial separation and hierarchical structuring of racial encounters whenever they occurred.

A pivotal requirement of my childhood education was to learn the language of racism, rendered explicit through the signs posted above water fountains, on toilets, inside buses, on dressing rooms. Learning to read and write thus involved the acquisition of an extensive familiarity with the protocols of racism during the pre–civil rights era. This was, in part, enabled by the fact that my elementary and high schools were a part of what was called the Negro School System. The home my parents purchased was located on the border of a neighborhood zoned for black people. Local laws prohibited us from crossing the street in front of our house, for we might be legally charged with trespassing into the white zone.

I mention these details because the U.S. civil rights movement, which took shape in the mid-1950s, contested these and other aspects of legalized racial segregation. As we demanded legal equality with respect to public transportation, housing, education, and the vote, we claimed the rights of citizenship, as they were capable of being provided by the law. The attainment of these rights of citizenship also involved a sustained struggle against lynching, which, since the end of the Civil War, had served as a brutal symbolic affirmation of white supremacy.

As the ideas of racial equality produced in and through the civil rights movement gradually acquired hegemony in the nation, they congealed into firm notions of what counted as victories over racial subjugation, and in the process produced their own meanings of racism. As important as these victories have proved to be, the inflexibility of the resulting definitions of racism has created, both in legal and popular discourses, enduring deceptions regarding the nature of racism. Definitions of racism informed by particular historical conditions became trans- or ahistorical ways of conceptualizing racial discrimination and subjugation. The persistence of these meanings beyond the particular historical conditions that produced them has hampered the evolution of a new vocabulary and new discourse that might allow us to identify new modes of racism in what is known as the post–civil rights era.

That the International Human Rights Community has recognized some of these new modes of racism was indicated in the title of the 2001 Durban, South Africa, World Conference Against Racism, Racist Discrimination, Xenophobia, and Related Intolerances. Regrettably, media coverage of the September 11 attacks in New York and Washington, which occurred at the end of the conference, resulted in sparse media attention to the aftermath of the World Conference. More public conversations about the conference might have helped to popularize more capacious meanings of racism.

Within the United States, scholars and activists have pointed out the perils of basing theories of racism, as well as anti-racist practices, on the black-white paradigm that informed the quest for civil rights and, further, of assuming that the civil rights paradigm is foundational to the very meaning of anti-racism. Neither paradigm can account, for example, for the role colonization and genocide against indigenous people played in shaping U.S. racism. The historical genocide against indigenous people relies precisely on invisibility—on an obstinate refusal to recognize the very existence of native North Americans, or a recognition or misrecognition that only acknowledges them as impediments to the transformation of the landscape—impediments to be destroyed or assimilated.

Differently racialized populations in the United States—First Nations, Mexican, Asian, and more recently people of Middle Eastern and South Asian descent—have been targets of different modes of racial subjugation. Islamophobia draws on and complicates what we know as racism. Moreover, racism, as it affects people of African descent, is today more deeply inflected by class, gender, and sexuality than we may have recognized it to be at the middle of the twentieth century.

The question I want to explore in this talk then is this: How does the persistence of historical meanings of racism and its remedies prevent us from recognizing the complex ways in which racism clandestinely structures prevailing institutions, practices, and ideologies in this era of neoliberalism?

Elizabeth Martínez, a legendary civil rights and Chicano movement activist, has pointed out, along with her collaborator Arnoldo García of the National Network of Immigrant and Refugee Rights, that the new conditions that constitute neoliberalism and characterize economic development since the 1980s involve an almost total freedom of movement for capital, goods, and services—in other words, the absolute rule of the market. Public expenditures for social services have been drastically cut. There has been constant pressure for the elimination of government intervention and regulation of the market. Thus the privatization of gas and electricity, of health care, education and many other human services has emerged as the mode of increased profits for global corporations. Finally,

Martínez and García point out, the concept of the public good and the very concept of "community" are being eliminated to make way for the notion of "individual responsibility." This results in "pressuring the poorest people in a society to find solutions to their lack of health care, education, and social security all by themselves—then blaming them if they fail, as 'lazy.'"[3]

I would add yet another point to this definition of neoliberalism: the flawed assumption that history does not matter. This idea, formulated by Francis Fukuyama as "The End of History," also involves, as Dinesh D'Souza put it, "The End of Racism." Both race and racism are profoundly historical. Thus if we discard biological and thus essentialist notions of "race" as fallacious, it would be erroneous to assume that we can also willfully extricate ourselves from histories of race and racism. Whether we acknowledge it or not, we continue to inhabit these histories, which help to constitute our social and psychic worlds.

Neoliberalism sees the market as the very paradigm of freedom, and democracy emerges as a synonym for capitalism, which has reemerged as the telos of history. In the official narratives of U.S. history, the historical victories of civil rights are dealt with as the final consolidation of democracy in the United States, having relegated racism to the dustbin of history. The path toward the complete elimination of racism is represented in the neoliberalist discourse of "color-blindness" and the assertion that equality can only be achieved when the law, as well as individual subjects, become blind to race. This approach, however, fails to apprehend the material and ideological work that race continues to do.

When obvious examples of racism appear to the public, they are considered to be isolated aberrations, to be addressed as anachronistic attributes of individual behavior. There have been a number of such cases in recent months in the United

States. I mention the noose that was hung on a tree branch by white students at a school in Jena, Louisiana, as a sign that black students were prohibited from gathering under that tree. I can also allude to the public use of racist expletives by a well-known white comedian, the racist and misogynist language employed by a well-known radio host in referring to black women on a college basketball team, and finally, recent comments regarding the golfer Tiger Woods.

Perhaps I should elaborate on this final example: Two sports journalists were recently involved in a conversation regarding the seemingly unstoppable Tiger Woods in relation to the new generation of golfers, who are having great difficulty catching up with him. One journalist noted that the younger golfers would probably have to get together and gang up on Woods. The other responded by saying that they would have to catch him and "lynch him in a back alley," thus conjuring, with a single casual phrase, a vast repressed history of ruthless racist violence.

These comments were, of course, readily identified as familiar—exceedingly familiar—expressions of attitudinal racism that are now treated as anachronistic expressions that were once articulated with state-sponsored racisms. Such occurrences are now relegated to the private sphere and only become *public* when they are literally *publicized*. Whereas, during an earlier period in our history, such comments would have been clearly understood as linked to state policy and to the material practices of social institutions, they are now treated as individual and private irregularities, to be solved by punishing and reeducating the individual by teaching them color-blindness, by teaching them not to notice the phenomenon of race.

But if we see these individual eruptions of racism as connected to the persistence and further entrenchment of institutional and structural racism that hides behind the curtain of neoliberalism, their meanings cannot be understood as individual aberrations. In the cases we have discussed, the racism is explicit and blatant. There is no denying that these are racist utterances. What happens, however, when racism is expressed not through the words of individuals, but rather through institutional practices that are "mute," to borrow the term Dana-Ain Davis uses, with respect to racism?[4]

The inability to recognize the contemporary persistence of racisms within institutions and other social structures results in the attribution of responsibility for the effects of racisms to the individuals who are its casualties, thus further exacerbating the problem of failing to identify the economic, social, and ideological work of racism. There is a similar logic undergirding the criminalization of those communities, which are vastly overrepresented in jails and prisons. By failing to recognize the material forces of racism that are responsible for offering up such large numbers of black and Latino youth to the carceral state, the process of criminalization imputes responsibility to the individuals who are its casualties, thus reproducing the very conditions that produce racist patterns in incarceration and its seemingly infinite capacity to expand. The misreading of these racist patterns replicates and reinforces the privatization that is at the core of neoliberalism, whereby social activity is individualized and the enormous profits generated by the punishment industry are legitimized.

On February 28, 2008, the Pew Center issued a report about incarceration in the United States titled "One in One Hundred: Behind Bars in America 2008." According to the report, one in one hundred adults is now behind bars on any given day. While the numbers themselves are shocking, the vastly disproportionate numbers of people of color in jails and prison is for the most part responsible for the figure "one in one hundred." According to the report: "For some groups, the incarceration numbers are especially startling. While one in 30 men between the ages of 20 and 34 is behind bars, for black males in that age group the figure is one in nine. Gender adds another dimension to the picture. Men still are roughly 10 times more likely to be in jail or prison, but the female population is burgeoning at a far brisker pace. For black women in their mid to late 30s, the incarceration rate also has hit the 1-in-100 mark."[5]

Parenthetically, when I recently mentioned these new figures to a group in London, including members of Parliament, almost everyone thought that either I had misspoken or that they had misheard me. As it turns out, they were familiar with the figures regarding the incarceration of young black men and were not so surprised that immense numbers of people of color were in jail. But it was difficult for them to grasp the idea that, given a majority white population, one in every one hundred adults in the United States is behind bars.

In 1985, there were fewer than 800,000 people behind bars. Today there are almost three times as many imprisoned people, and the vast increase has been driven almost entirely by the practice of incarcerating young people of color. Although the figures are not comparable, one can argue that a similar dynamic drives imprisonment here in Australia, with imprisoned Aboriginal people accounting for ten times their proportion in the general population.

Why, then, is it so difficult to name these practices as racist? Why does the word "racist" have such an archaic ring to it, as if we were caught in a time warp? Why is it so difficult to name the crisis in imprisonment as a crisis of racism?

According to the Pew Report: "The United States incarcerates more people than any country in the world, including the far more populous nation of China. At the start of the new year, the American penal system held more than 2.3 million adults. China was second, with 1.5 million people behind bars, and Russia was a distant third with 890,000 inmates, according to the latest available figures. Beyond the sheer number of inmates, America also is the global leader in the rate at which it incarcerates its citizenry, outpacing nations like South Africa and Iran. In Germany, 93 people are in prison for every 100,000 adults and children. In the U.S, the rate is roughly eight times that, or 750 per 100,000."

These figures have been produced by the vastly disproportionate numbers of youth of color, especially young black men, who are currently behind bars. For example, if one out of every sixty white men between the ages of 20 and 24 is behind bars, then one of out every nine black men of the same age is incarcerated. According to neoliberalist explanations, the fact that these young black men are behind bars has little to do with race or racism and everything to do with their own private family upbringing and their inability to take moral responsibility for their actions. Such explanations remain "mute"—to use Dana-Ain Davis's term again—about the social, economic, and historical power of racism. They remain "mute" about the dangerous contemporary work that race continues to do.

The incarceration of youth of color—and of increasing numbers of young women of color—is not viewed as connected to the vast structural changes produced by deregulation, privatization, by the devaluation of the public good, and by the deterioration of community. Because there is no public vocabulary that allows us to place these developments within a historical context, individual deviancy is the overarching explanation for the grotesque rise in the numbers of people who are relegated to the country's and the world's prisons. According to Henry Giroux, "racism survives through the guise of neoliberalism, a kind of repartee that imagines human agency as simply a matter of individualized choices, the only obstacle to effective citizenship and agency being the lack of principled self-help and moral responsibility."[6]

Because racism is viewed as an anachronistic vestige of the past, we fail to grasp the extent to which the long memory of institutions—especially those that constitute the intimately connected circuit of education and incarceration—continue to permit race to determine who has access to education and who has access to incarceration. While laws have had the effect of privatizing racist attitudes and eliminating the explicitly racist practices of institutions, these laws are unable to apprehend the deep structural life of racism and therefore allow it to continue to thrive.

This invisible work of racism not only influences the life chances of millions of people, it helps to nourish a psychic reservoir of racism that often erupts through the utterances and actions of individuals, as in the cases previously mentioned. The frequent retort made by such individuals who are caught in the act—"I'm not a racist. I don't even know where that came from"—can only be answered if we are able to recognize this deep structural life of racism.

The deep structural racism of the criminal justice system affects our lives in complicated ways. What we acknowledged more than a decade ago as the U.S. prison-industrial complex through which racism generates enormous profits for private corporations, can now be recognized as a global prison-industrial complex that profits the world over from postcolonial forms of racism and xenophobia. With the dismantling of the welfare state and the structural adjustment in the southern region required by global financial institutions, the institution of the prison—which is itself an important product marketed through global capitalism—becomes the privileged site into which surplus impoverished populations are deposited. Thus new forms of global structural racism are emerging. The deep structural life of racism bleeds out from the U.S. criminal justice system and is having a devastating effect on the political life of the nation and the world.

Since the era of slavery, racism has been associated with death. Geographer Ruth Gilmore has defined racism as "the state-sanctioned and/or legal production and exploitation of group-diferentiated vulnerabilities to premature death, in distinct yet densely interconnected political geographies."[7] The death to which Gilmore refers is multidimensional, embracing corporeal death, social death, and civil death. From its advent, the institution of the prison has been organically liked to the political order of democracy in that it negatively demonstrates the centrality of individual rights and liberties. Civil life is negated and the prisoner is relegated to the status of civil death. Following Claude Meillassoux and Orlando Patterson, Colin (Joan) Dayan and other scholars have compared the social death of slavery to the civil death of imprisonment, particularly given the landmark legal case *Ruffin v. Commonwealth*, which in 1871 declared the prisoner to be "the slave of the state."

Although prisoners' state of civil death has now mutated so that they are no longer the living dead, as Dayan characterized them—that is to say, their residual rights have been slightly augmented—there remains a range of deprivations that situate the prisoner, and indeed also the ex-prisoner, beyond the boundaries of liberal democracy.

In the time that remains, I want to look at one such deprivation—the loss of the right to vote—and would like to think about the impact of felon disenfranchisement as a by-product of racism in the workings of contemporary U.S. democracy.

In the United States, imprisoned populations, except in the states of Vermont and Maine, lose the franchise either temporarily or permanently. This means that 5.3 million people have lost their right to vote, either permanently or temporarily. Among black men, the figures are even more dramatic: almost two million black men, or 13 percent of the total population of black adult men. In some states, one out of every four black men, is barred from voting.

The historical period which witnessed a significant expansion of felon disenfranchisement laws was the post–Civil War era, in other words after the passage of the Fourteenth and Fifteenth Amendments. In fact, just as the Thirteenth Amendment, which legally (and only legally) ended slavery, designated convicts as exceptions; the Fourteenth Amendment, which guaranteed all persons equal protection of the law also contained an exception—Section 2 permitted states to withdraw suffrage rights from those who were engaged in "rebellion or other crimes."[8]

According to Elizabeth Hull, Southern constitutional conventions during the period following the overthrow of Radical Reconstruction—to use W. E. B. DuBois's periodization—developed strategies of criminalization precisely to divest former slaves and their descendants of the right to vote. Many Southern states passed laws that linked those crimes that were specifically associated with black people to disenfranchisement, while those associated with white people did not result in withdrawal of the right to vote. In states such as Mississippi, there was the ironic situation that if you were convicted of murder you retained your voting rights, but if convicted of miscegenation, you lost your right to vote.[9]

Jeff Manza and Christoper Uggen's work find that between 1850 and 2002, states with larger proportions of people of color in their prison populations were more likely to pass laws restricting their right to vote, which leads them to conclude that there is a "direct connection between racial politics and felon disenfranchisement. . . . When we ask the question of how we got to the point where American practice can be so out of line with the rest of the world," they write, "the most plausible answer we can supply is that of race."[10]

It can be confidently argued that the Bush presidency was enabled precisely by the relegation of a large, majority black population of "free" individuals to the status of civil death. George W. Bush "won" the Florida elections in 2000 by a tiny margin of 537 votes. As Congressman John Conyers has pointed out, the fact that 600,000 ex-felons were denied participation in the elections in the state of Florida alone "may have literally changed the history of this nation."[11] We might thus argue that the deep structural life of racism in the U.S. prison system gave us the president who articulated the collective fears linked to a psychic historical reservoir of racism in order to wage wars on the peoples of Afghanistan and Iraq under the guise of combating terror.

ELEVEN

Democracy, Social Change, and Civil Engagement

Bryn Mawr College, Pennsylvania
February 2, 2009

Thank you for inviting me to speak here at Bryn Mawr during your celebration of Black History Month.

As everyone is aware, this is a very special moment in the history of our country—the only Black History Month that will have been celebrated in the immediate aftermath of the election, for the first time, of a black president who identifies with the black radical tradition of struggle for freedom. It has been barely two weeks since the inauguration of Barack Hussein Obama, which means that the experience of having a president willing to make bold progressive moves is still very new.

But you have asked me to speak on the topic: "Democracy, Social Change, and Civil Engagement."

In pursuing this question, I want to first examine the most extreme proposition that has emerged during this period of celebrating the ascendancy of Barack Obama to the U.S. presidency. Many people have said that Martin King's dream has been realized. They have said that the very last barrier of racism has been overcome. They say that a black person can be anything! This must mean that U.S. democracy has reached a zenith, that change has come to America, that the dream has been realized.

Could it be that a black man is elected to the presidency, and all the barriers of racism come crashing down? Some mainstream media appear to think so. According to the *New York Times*, for example, Obama managed to "sweep away the last racial barrier in American politics with ease as the country chose him as its first black chief executive."

The election of Barack Obama may not be such an extraordinary phenomenon for young people who have been shaped by popular visual culture. How many black presidents have they already experienced? Dennis Haysbert was president in *Twenty-Four*; Morgan Freeman, Danny Glover, and others have also been cast in the role.

But where is the logic here? A black man is now the president and commander in chief of the United States of America. All people who suffer the effects of discrimination according to race, gender, sexuality, disability, etc., have experienced progress; but have they been magically released from the conditions of their subjugation?

So what is the significance of Obama's election?

Something quite earthshaking has occured—but it is not that the Obama presidency can miraculously transform the material conditions of poor people, black people, other people of color, immigrants, gays, lesbians, bisexuals, transgender and intersex people. It has not brought liberation to us. But it does tell us what kind of political and ideological environment we now inhabit. It tells us something about this historical conjuncture.

The election of Barack Obama did not prevent a BART police officer in Oakland, California, from shooting an unarmed black youth. But it does give us hope that we have a more hospitable terrain for the struggle against police violence.

What many of us used to call the "Other America," the America descended from Harriet Tubman and John Brown, from Rosa Parks, Martin Luther King, and Cesar Chavez, and Joe Hill, and the Haymarket martyrs, the America that historically experienced slavery and colonization and economic exploitation, that Invisible America is finally the America that can potentially provide the leadership we need during these difficult times.

Let us say it loudly and proudly: *President Barack Hussein Obama.*

I do not want to gloss over the challenges of the moment. In fact, I do not think I would be respecting the import of Black History Month that we celebrate if I portrayed this election and this inauguration as the panacea to all our problems. But I do want us to relish this victory, to celebrate this moment, this historical conjuncture, to ride for a moment the wave of collective, global emotional solidarities occasioned by this triumph. I want us to relish it, not for what it portends, not for its consequences, but for what it means at this moment in history. For what it means to generations of people of African descent, generations of people of all racial and ethnic backgrounds here and abroad who learned how to place justice, equality, and peace before economic profit, before ideologies of racism.

Many people assume that the current election represents the final victory of the civil rights movement. So let me talk about civil rights.

As we all know, the term "civil rights" refers to the rights of citizens, of all citizens, but because the very nature of citizenship in the United States has always been troubled by the refusal to grant citizenship to subordinate groups—indigenous people, African slaves, women of all racial and economic backgrounds—we tend to think of some people as model citizens, as archetypical citizens, those whose civil rights are never placed in question, the quintessential citizens, and others as having to wage struggles for the right to be regarded as citizens. And some—undocumented immigrants or "suspected" undocumented immigrants, along with ex-felons or "suspected" ex-felons—are beyond the reach of citizenship altogether.

We still live with this two-tiered notion of citizenship.

The punishment of imprisonment is predicated on the assumption that people have rights and liberties that can be taken away from them. Think about a photographic positive and negative—the prison is the negative of the larger liberal democracy.

Because of the long history of black people's campaigns for equality, the term "civil rights" has become a synonym for those legal measures that assure racial equality. Because the history of the quest for "civil rights" dates back to slavery, there has been a tendency to assume that black people are the representative subjects of "civil rights" and that "civil rights" are affirmed through legislative and judicial processes, which attempt to assure racial equality before the law.

We all know that here in the United States, black people are not the only ones who have been denied full rights of citizenship. Other racialized communities have been and continue to be denied citizenship; full rights of citizenship are denied by virtue of gender and by virtue of sexuality. Some people react negatively when they hear about the struggle for the civil rights of LGBT communities regarding things like the right to marry (and this tells us nothing about the patriarchal and heterosexist nature of the institution of marriage itself).

The problems that emerge from this tendency to equate civil rights with African American subjects are many. For example, during the 2008 presidential campaign, I was struck by the racially inflected anxiety that emerged among McCain-Palin supporters and by the discourse of citizenship that drives it. During one of the televised McCain-Palin rallies in Minnesota, a woman said: "I can't trust Obama. I have read about him and he's not, he's not uh—he's an Arab." At this point, McCain took the microphone from her and said: "No ma'am. He's a decent family man [and] citizen that I just happen to have disagreements with on fundamental issues and that's what this campaign's all about."

Why did it not even occur to McCain to say that although Obama is not an Arab, there would be nothing wrong with an Arab running for the presidency? If you consider the woman's rather incoherent remark, she could have just have easily substituted "Negro" at a different historical moment, or "Jew."

But the point is this: In his response, McCain implied that had he really been an Arab, he could not have been characterized as a "decent family man," he could not have been characterized as a "citizen." Embedded in his response was the notion that Arabs are excluded from U.S. citizenship as well as discourses of heterosexism, that citizenship itself is racialized and sexualized. It would be interesting to consider how the word "decent" has come to stand in for the differentiation of those who would otherwise be associated with criminalized communities. Therefore, while poor black communities are still systematically criminalized, there are those who have risen "above race" and are therefore "decent."

I am extremely concerned that Obama has not found a way to challenge the anti-Arab racism and the implicit Islamophobia.

But it is important that he gave his first interview to *Al Arabiya*.

We are celebrating Black History Month. Revisit what is now officially known as the civil right era, and let us invoke the Freedom Movement for which Dr. King gave his life—especially all those—like Fannie Lou Hamer, Rev. Ralph Abernathy, James Foreman, Dorothy Smith Robinson, Ella Baker, and Joanne Robinson—who did not live to see this day.

They did not know what they were unleashing; they believed so strongly in justice, and equality, and in their own collective ability to eradicate an important structure of racism in Alabama, Georgia, Mississippi, that they inspired people all over the South, all over the country, and throughout the world.

Fifty years ago, the evocation of "race" by drum majors for justice (as Dr. King called them) signified equality, hope, and change. Of course, when it was raised by believers in segregation forever, it represented the status quo.

Today, many aspects of our society have changed. It is not the same world I knew as a child growing up some nine miles from here in Birmingham, when I was horrified to hear about Emmett Till, and overjoyed to hear about the boycott.

Change has come in some respects, as Obama himself pointed out in his speech on race, yet racism is far from fully eradicated. Why, then, was it so difficult to have a sustained conversation on race during the election campaign? Why did "race" signify negativity, why did it signify chaos? Why was it not possible to pursue some of the questions that Obama himself raised?

The work that race does—the work that it has done historically, and the central place it occupies in the collective psyche of this country—is very complex and has many dimensions. But in all this, perhaps its historical dimension is most central.

We live in a country whose population has not acquired the habit of taking historical memory seriously. And therefore we tend to assume that something that happened ten years ago or twenty or thirty years ago is a part of a history that remains securely in the past.

But histories never leave us for another inaccessible place. They are a part of us; they inhabit us and we inhabit them even when we are not aware of this relationship to history.

In his now famous speech on race, Obama identifies with the historical struggles against racism, and I think this is what has generated so much excitement across generations and across racial and ethnic identifications.

If we have discarded anachronistic notions of race that are grounded in pseudoscientific classifications of humanity that are hierarchal by their very nature, if we have discarded these notions of race, we cannot discard the work that race has done to shape our histories.

So many of us have said that we did not expect to see a black president in our lifetimes. This phrase has been repeated so many times, especially by people of African descent, that I think we should stop and reflect on its meaning.

We are primarily referring to people of a certain generation who have said that they did not think they would live to see this day (although Martin Luther King said in the 1960s that it should take not forty, but twenty-five years).

How many times have you heard someone say, "I didn't think I would see an African American president in my lifetime." That a black president was indeed elected was so momentous that huge numbers of people were drawn to Washington to witness for themselves, or at least on the big screens on the mall—the swearing in of President Barack Obama.

How do we define "black" or "African American"? Our

definition is a political one; it is one that is first and foremost associated with the struggle for freedom. The meaning of blackness in historical context is inexorably linked to the meaning of freedom—to the meaning of democracy.

If the black person elected had not identified with these struggles, with the authentic expansion of freedom in the country and the world, if the black person had been a Clarence Thomas–type figure, then I do not think we would have responded in the same way. If there had been a black candidate who vowed to continue the Iraq War, who placed the needs of corporations over those of people, who wanted to continue the old Bush policies, then we would not have responded in the same way.

Orlando Patterson points out in his monumental study of slavery that freedom was first imagined and invented by slaves; it was first imagined by those whose lives were the negation of freedom.

So let us remember enslaved women and men who imagined and struggle for freedom. Let us remember the many activists in the 1930s and 1940s who paved the way for the freedom struggle of the 1950s and 1960s, those who dared to imagine a better place, a better world.

We have heard Obama talk about the economic crisis and we have heard him make a commitment to move boldly and firmly. We have heard him commit to ending the war in Iraq, but I am not so sure we need an accelerated war in Afghanistan. We have heard Obama say that our public safety should not require the sacrifice of our principles and ideals. And we expect that the military prison at Guantánamo will soon be shut down. And we expect him to move swiftly to save the planetary environment.

But I also want to hear Obama commit to ending racial profiling and police violence. And we need to develop strategies that do not require us to reinvent the wheel every time a young person is killed by the police.

I want to hear Obama commit to ending the imprisonment binge. There are more than two million people behind bars, many only because they are young and black or Latino and poor. If there is a commitment to fix the educational system, there must also be a commitment to abolish the existing prison system.

Racism has not ended because one black man now occupies the highest office of the land, or because one black family is in the White House. As we celebrate their ascendancy, let us not forget the millions of families that have been disrupted because of the institutional racism that structures the criminal justice system.

Obama has committed to a new policy toward the Muslim world. In supporting him in that venture, we ask that he acknowledge the violence and oppression that has been visited upon our Palestinian sisters and brothers—especially now those who live in Gaza.

Bishop Gene Robinson's Prayer

Bless us with tears — for a world in which over a billion people exist on less than a dollar a day, where young women from many lands are beaten and raped for wanting an education, and thousands die daily from malnutrition, malaria, and AIDS.

Bless us with anger — at discrimination, at home and abroad, against refugees and immigrants, women, people of color, gay, lesbian, bisexual and transgender people.

Bless us with discomfort — at the easy, simplistic "answers" we've preferred to hear from our politicians, instead of the truth, about ourselves and the world, which we need to face if we are going to rise to the challenges of the future.

Bless us with patience — and the knowledge that none of what ails us will be "fixed" anytime soon, and the understanding that our new president is a human being, not a messiah.

Bless us with humility — open to understanding that our own needs must always be balanced with those of the world.

Bless us with freedom from mere tolerance — replacing it with a genuine respect and warm embrace of our differences, and an understanding that in our diversity, we are stronger.

TWELVE

Difficult Dialogues

National Women's Studies Association Conference, Atlanta
November 12, 2009

One of the organizations with which I work and which has served as the terrain on which some of the collective insights I will share with you have grown is Sisters Inside, an abolitionist organization that focuses on women in prison. Attending meetings and conferences in Australia, where Sisters Inside is headquartered, I have learned that before anything else can proceed, we always acknowledge the traditional holders of the land.

Here in Atlanta, Georgia, I want to acknowledge the original inhabitants and holders of the land on which we gather this evening, recognizing that Native men and women have been and continue to be the most consistently excluded from circles of justice. I have vowed to myself to make this ceremonial acknowledgement each time I speak at a public gathering in order not to assent to the discursive genocide that continues to affirm the genocide of colonization.

It has been thirty-two years since the founding of the National Women's Studies Association (NWSA). For those of us who have been teaching and writing in and around the fields of women's and gender studies, of feminist studies for the duration of the NWSA's existence, it is very difficult to believe that it has been more than three decades since the founding conference. My first formal affiliation with Women's Studies was the same year as that conference, 1977, and I am feeling very nostalgic about those years at San Francisco State when Cherríe Moraga and Gloria Anzaldúa and bell hooks were among my colleagues.

There were times when I would have found it virtually impossible to imagine that the NWSA would be presided over by a black woman—much less a black woman like Beverly Guy-Sheftall. (The theme of this conference is "Difficult Dialogues." This, however, is something I don't find it difficult to say).

When I discovered that Beverly had been elected president of the NWSA, I experienced a shudder of delight, the kind of shudder that initiates a shift from one dimension to another. This is historic; this is equivalent to a millennial shift for the feminist studies community; hopefully this marks the beginning of a new era.

How can we best open a conference whose theme is difficult dialogues?

Today, we will examine how feminist intellectual, political, and institutional practices cannot be adequately practiced if the politics of gender are conceptualized (overtly or implicitly) as superseding or transcending the politics of race, sexuality, social class, nation, and disability.

For many years and many decades, there have been critiques of, and struggles against, those who insisted that gender as a category was self-contained and self-sufficient and that scholarly inquiry into the construction of gender was possible without attending to race, sexuality, class, disability, and nation.

This conference reflects a new consensus, or at least the desire for a new consensus, around a complex of issues that have been the source of a debate that has lasted well over a century.

In their book *Gender Talk*, Beverly Guy-Sheftall and Johnnetta Cole remind us that two decades after the putative end of slavery, Anna Julia Cooper was calling for "a moment of retrospection, introspection, and prospection" in order to analyze, in their words, "the pervasive legacy of slavery," "the racism of the white women's movement," and an "analysis of sexism within the Black community."

These debates have unfolded at earlier NWSA conferences, for example, at the famous 1983 Storrs, Connecticut, conference, written about by Gloria Bowles and Chela Sandoval, whose theme was "Women Respond to Racism."

There has been a long history of attempting to figure out how to think and act upon these categories as intersectional, but not always neatly intersecting, rather as overlaying and crosshatched.

As Beverly and Johnnetta point out in their book, this history extends from Anna Julia Cooper's early efforts through Pauli Murray's pairing of Jim Crow and Jane Crow to Frances Beal's Double Jeopardy to the Third World Women's Alliance's Triple Jeopardy.

The most important message, which we have also learned from the work of Chandra Mohanty and Jacqui Alexander, is that we can never assume that the category "women" equally represents all women. [There are] hierarchies of race and class, and now that we have begun to challenge the binary assumptions behind gender, we can say hierarchies of gender as well. Where, for example, does a transgender woman figure into the hierarchy?

And feminism is still a contested term—this is perhaps what revitalizes it from one generation to the next. For those of you who have problems with the label, I can tell the story of being interpellated into feminism when I published *Women, Race, and Class*.

My first response was: *Feminist? Who, me? No, not me. I am a black women who identifies with the struggles of the working class.* But after a while I did answer the hail. I became more and more comfortable with the idea of identifying into feminism. I saw the category itself becoming larger and roomier, encompassing and embracing historical contributions of women of color and refiguring and refashioning itself in response to critical engagements of those who insisted that feminism be anti-racist, and also in solidarity with the struggles of working-class women of all racial and ethnic backgrounds, and that it be transnational in scope.

The reach of the category is constantly expanding, but it also narrows. That queer theory incorporates, but also contests, some instantiations of feminist theory is one example. And queer-of-color theory attempts to build on the contributions of women-of-color feminist theory. And just as feminism implicitly accepted, in the beginning at least, the binary structure of gender, it has had to respond to the critiques of the binarism that emanate from the very interesting transgender, intersex, and gender-nonconforming theories and activism, which in turn have had to engage with intersectionalities of race and class.

I could go on and on spinning what appears to be a labyrinth of ideas that is so complex that it makes our heads hurt. Why can't it be simple? If we were only to focus on gender, it would make things so much easier. But of course, it has been this yearning toward simplicity that has racialized feminism as white, that has been responsible for its false universals.

On the other hand, it is the very capacity of feminism to

embrace more and more complexity in response to historical circumstances that renders it so exciting. This is what renders it so radical. This is what keeps the field in a perpetual state of instability, sometimes verging on crisis. This instability and these crises should not be eschewed. Instability and crisis can be productive if we are willing to dwell within the interstices of the instabilities.

Feminism is concerned with women; feminism is concerned with gender; feminism is concerned with sexuality and race. But there may be something more important that those particular objects of our concern. Feminist methodologies, both for research and for organizing, impel us to explore connections that are not always apparent, they drive us to inhabit contradictions and discover what is productive in these contradictions and methods of thought and action; they urge us to think things together that appear to be entirely separate and to disaggregate things that appear to belong naturally together.

Feminist methods, both in research and in organizing for social justice, require us to challenge the singularity, the separateness, and the wholeness of a range of social categories.

I marvel at our ability to conceptualize and formulate that which was without a name, that which was inchoate, that which provoked strong emotional responses in us at one time, but we could not easily talk about the racing of gender and the gendering of race.

Those of us who have been around for a while and are accustomed to older vocabularies should welcome the new ideas, new formulations, new vocabularies. Here we should pay tribute to all the young scholars who want to change the field and who want to change the world!

I promised Beverly that I would say a few words about my own intellectual development, so I decided to read a section of the introduction to a new edition of Frederick Douglass's *Narrative* that also includes the very first lectures I gave as an assistant professor of Philosophy at UCLA:

"When I first read Douglass's *Narrative*, I had not yet learned how to recognize the extent to which the equivalence of "freedom" and "manhood" meant that women were excluded by definition from enjoying the full benefits of freedom. In fact, today I find it simultaneously somewhat embarrassing to realize that my UCLA lectures on Douglass rely on an implicitly masculinist notion of freedom, and exciting to realize how much we have matured with respect to feminist analysis since that period. Thanks to my training in German philosophy, I had acquired conceptual tools that allowed me to analyze the complex trajectories from bondage to freedom (using, for example Hegel's approach to the relationship between master and slave in *The Phenomenology of Mind*), but it was not until I began to work on "The Black Women's Role in the Community of Slaves" (a year later during the time I was imprisoned) that I began to recognize the fundamental importance of developing gender analyses.

"As I revisit the lectures that accompany this current edition of Frederick Douglass's *Narrative*, I am surprised by how much I did not know at the beginning of an era that witnessed the rise of Black Studies and Women's/Feminist Studies. In 1969, when I was hired by UCLA's Department of Philosophy to teach courses in Continental Philosophy, I welcomed the opportunity to teach courses in the tradition forged by Kant, Hegel, and Marx. Such courses would allow me to put to good use my training as a student of Herbert Marcuse and Theodor Adorno. But I was also deeply interested in the emergence of Black Studies—at UCLA, the Center for Afro-American Studies was founded shortly before I joined the Philosophy faculty—and wanted my teaching to incorporate these new developments. At that time there was no available body of literature on black philosophy, nor was there a significant group of philosophy scholars who worked on issues of race and ethnicity. Consequently I decided to design a course that I called "Recurring Philosophical Themes in Black Literature" that would entail examining black literary texts with the aim of identifying the major philosophical questions they posed.

"The overarching question I considered in the course was that of liberation. I intended to think about liberation both in broad philosophical terms and in the way the theme of liberation is embedded in the literary history of black people in North America. Although current events were beyond the scope of the course, I expected the students to take note of the wide-ranging engagements with theories and practices of liberation in movement circles. After all, it was 1969, barely a year and a half since the assassination of Dr. Martin Luther King, which had rekindled popular discussion and organizing around strategies of liberation. Internecine strife within the black youth movement pitted cultural nationalists against socialists and internationalists, and it had been a little less than a year since Black Panther leaders John Huggins and Bunchy Carter were killed by members of the cultural nationalist association known as US Organization during a Black Student Union meeting on the UCLA campus. Moreover, I, myself, had been under intense political pressure since California Governor Ronald Reagan and the Regents of the University of California had announced shortly before I began to teach that they were firing me because of my membership in the Communist Party USA. I taught this course on philosophy and black literature while seeking and eventually receiving a court ruling enjoining the Regents from firing me based on my political affiliation.

"I should point out that even though there was no formal incorporation of gender analyses into my first courses, my activist experiences involved intense battles over the role of women in such black community organizations as the Student Nonviolent Coordinating Committee and the Black Panther Party. The patriarchal structure of the cultural nationalist US Organization left no space for contestation. Moreover, I had personally come under attack by some members of the community who did not think that I deserved to take a leadership position given the fact that I was a woman."

The approach to the question of liberation I pursued in "Recurring Philosophical Themes in Black Literature" linked philosophical understandings of freedom with histories of black political struggle and cultural production as they resonated with contemporary efforts to extend and enlarge the meaning of freedom. What better text to begin with than Frederick Douglass's autobiography? Students would follow a trajectory from bondage to liberty that would help them to better apprehend the nature of freedom as forged by those who have had most at stake in the struggle for liberation. The first two lectures—based on rough transcripts of my remarks, which referred to the later autobiography, *The Life and Times of Frederick Douglass*—accompany this edition of Frederick Douglass's *Narrative*. They are published here in the form in which they were circulated in 1970 after I was arrested on charges of murder, kidnapping, and conspiracy, and included a strong letter of support from faculty members at UCLA. When I taught this course, I did not realize that less than a year later, I would be in jail awaiting trial on three capital charges.

Just as I designed a course that reflected the influence of the raging movements for black liberation—and for the liberation of all racially oppressed communities, my first published article and my first conference paper were directly influenced by my experiences in the movement. I wrote "Black Women's Role" as a response to popularization of the Moynihan report among black men (and women) in movement circles.

Why do I mention this? Because I think we should all be talking about producing knowledge that makes a difference.

This conference attests to the fact that we have come a very long way, but we still have a very long way to go.

Demand for women's studies, like demand for black studies, Chicano/Latino, Asian American, Native American studies, are linked to larger quest for equality, justice, freedom.

We are interested not in race and gender (and class and sexuality and disability) per se, by themselves, but primarily as they have been acknowledged as conditions for hierarchies of power, so that we can transform them into intertwined vectors of struggle for freedom.

When we identify into feminism, we mean new epistemologies, new ways of producing knowledge and transforming social relations.

As scholars and activists, we realize that categories always fall short of the social realities they attempt to represent, and social realities always exceed the categories that attempt to contain them.

This is why we keep changing our vocabularies.

I take the category "freedom" very seriously, and I realize how far we have to go before we can say that we have truly shifted freedom's terrain, especially when a young high school student is gang-raped, and the most widespread response is not *why didn't the onlookers intervene and stop the assault*, but rather, *why didn't they call the police.*

I realize how far we have to go when I consider that the Health Care Bill just passed by the House severely restricts federal funding for abortion procedures, i.e., no funding for abortions except in the cases of rape, incest, and when the life of the mother is threatened. Let's remember that the Hyde Amendment was passed in the same year that NWSA was founded. Moreover, any four-person family making $88K per year or less who would receive a U.S. government subsidy, would be prohibited from buying an insurance plan that covers abortions. Who do you think is going to suffer as a result?

We fight the same battles over and over again. They are never won for eternity, but in the process of struggling together, in community, we learn how to glimpse new possibilities that otherwise never would have become apparent to us, and in the process we expand and enlarge our very notion of freedom.

ENDNOTES

1. Two of her paradigm-shifting essays were written from prison, "Reflections on the Black Woman's Role in the Community of Slaves," and "Women and Capitalism: Dialectics of Oppression and Liberation," both reprinted in Joy James, ed., *The Angela Y. Davis Reader* (Hoboken, NJ: Wiley Blackwell, 1998), pp. 111–128, 161–192.
2. Howe Verhovek, Sam. "Air Passengers Vow to Resist Any Hijackers," *New York Times*, October 11, 2001.
3. Martínez, Elizabeth and Arnoldo García. "What is Neoliberalism? A Brief Definition for Activists,"/www.corpwatch.org/article.php?id=376
4. Davis, Dana-Ain. "Narrating the Mute: Racializing and Racism in a Neoliberal Moment," *Souls*, 9:4 (2007), pp. 34–360.
5. www.pewcenteronthestates.org
6. Giroux, Henry A. "Spectacles of Race and Pedagogies of Denial: Anti-Black Racist Pedagogy Under the Reign of Neoliberalism," *Communication Education*, 52:3 (2003), pp. 191–211.
7. Gilmore, Ruth Wilson. "Race and Globalization," In P.J. Taylor, R.L. Johnston, M.J. Watts, eds. *Geographies of Global Change*, 2nd edition (Oxford: Basil Blackwell, 2002), Ch. 17, p. 261.
8. Hull, Elizabeth A. *The Disenfranchisement of Ex-Felons* (Philadelphia: Temple University Press, 2006) p. 18.
9. Hull, p. 19.
10. Manza, Jeff and Uggen, Christopher; *Locked Out: Felon Disenfranchisement and American Democracy*, Oxford University Press, 2006, p. 68.
11. Hull, p. ix (Foreword).

ABOUT THE AUTHORS

ANGELA Y. DAVIS

Through her activism and her scholarship over the last decades, Angela Davis has been deeply involved in our nation's quest for social justice. Her work as an educator—both at the university level and in the larger public sphere—has always emphasized the importance of building communities of struggle for economic, racial, and gender equality.

Professor Davis's teaching career has taken her to San Francisco State University, Mills College, and UC Berkeley. She has also taught at UCLA, Vassar, the Claremont Colleges, and Stanford University. She spent the last fifteen years at the University of California Santa Cruz, where she is now Professor Emerita of History of Consciousness, an interdisciplinary PhD program, and of Feminist Studies.

Angela Davis is the author of eight books and has lectured throughout the United States as well as in Europe, Africa, Asia, Australia, and South America. In recent years a persistent theme of her work has been the range of social problems associated with incarceration and the generalized criminalization of those communities that are most affected by poverty and racial discrimination. She draws upon her own experiences in the early seventies as a person who spent eighteen months in jail and on trial, after being placed on the FBI's "Ten Most Wanted" list. She has also conducted extensive research on numerous issues related to race, gender, and imprisonment. Her most recent books are *Are Prisons Obsolete?*, *Abolition Democracy*, and a new critical edition of *Narrative of the Life of Frederick Douglass*, all published in the Open Media Series.

Angela Davis is a member of the executive board of the Women of Color Resource Center, a San Francisco Bay Area organization that emphasizes popular education—of and about women who live in conditions of poverty. She also works with Justice Now, which provides legal assistance to women in prison and engages in advocacy for the abolition of imprisonment as the dominant strategy for addressing social problems. Internationally, she is affiliated with Sisters Inside, a similar organization based in Queensland, Australia.

Like many other educators, Professor Davis is especially concerned with the general tendency to devote more resources and attention to the prison system than to educational institutions. Having helped to popularize the notion of a "prison-industrial complex," she now urges her audiences to think seriously about the future possibility of a world without prisons and to help forge a twenty-first-century abolitionist movement.

ROBIN D. G. KELLEY

Professor Kelley is a professor of History and American Studies and Ethnicity at the University of Southern California. From 2003 to 2006, he was the William B. Ransford Professor of Cultural and Historical Studies at Columbia University. From 1994 to 2003, he was a professor of history and Africana Studies at New York University and served as the chairman of NYU's history department from 2002 to 2003. One of the youngest tenured professors in a full academic discipline, attaining this status at the age of 32, Kelley has spent most of his career exploring American and African American history with a particular emphasis on African American musical culture, including jazz and hip hop. Kelley is also working on two other books: *Speaking in Tongues: Jazz and Modern Africa* and *A World to Gain: A History of African Americans*. His latest book is *Thelonious Monk: The Life and Times of an American Original*.

Open Media is a movement-oriented publishing project committed to the vision of "one world in which many worlds fit"—a world with social justice, democracy, and human rights for all people. Founded in 1991 by Greg Ruggiero, Open Media has a history of producing critically acclaimed and best-selling titles that address the most urgent political and social issues of our time.

City Lights Open Media Series
www.citylights.com/collections/openmedia/